GOLF

The Skills of the Game

Paul Ashwell

The Crowood Press

First published in 2001 by
The Crowood Press Ltd
Ramsbury, Marlborough
Wiltshire SN8 2HR

British Library Cataloguing-in-Publication Data
A catalogue record for this book is available from the British Library.

ISBN 1 86126 442 9

Dedication
To my wife Julie and children Ben and Annie.

Acknowledgements
I would like to take this opportunity to thank a number of people for
their contribution to this book: Keith Williams, English Golf Union
Head Coach; John Jacobs, President PGA of Europe, 1999–2001;
Dr Brian Hemmings, Senior Lecturer in Sport Psychology, University
College, Northampton; Steve Connolly, PGA Professional; Chris
Mayson, England Boys player; John Moffat, Cameo Photography;
The National Golf Centre, Woodhall Spa; John Hubbard for patiently
checking the text.

Photographs by John Moffat, Cameo Photography

Line drawings by Annette Findlay

Throughout this book the use of pronouns covers both males and
females. All technical information is directed towards right-handed
golfers (apologies to all left-handers!).

Typeset by Florence Production Ltd, Stoodleigh, Devon

Printed and bound in Great Britain by J. W. Arrowsmith Ltd.

Contents

Foreword

I am both delighted and honoured to be asked to pen a few words by way of foreword to this most comprehensive Golf Instructional Book by Paul Ashwell. I have no doubt it will benefit players of all levels: the skilled and the average, the illustrious and the humble. Newcomers to the game will particularly benefit from the early chapters on the rules, scoring and equipment.

I particularly like the importance Paul attaches to ball flight and the impact dimensions that have such an effect on this vital element of our game with both long and short game skills.

Similarly the chapter covering on-course situations is bound to be of benefit not only on the physical side of shot making, but also improving the mental attitude – so very necessary if we are to maximize our golfing technique.

The author has obviously put much time and effort into this most excellent work. I congratulate him and have no hesitation in recommending it to golfers of all levels.

John Jacobs, OBE
President, PGA of Europe 1999–2001
Member, US Teachers Hall of Fame
Ryder Cup Captain 1979 and 1981

ABOUT THE AUTHOR

Paul Ashwell is a PGA Professional who has been teaching people to play golf for twenty years. He is English Golf Union Boys Coach for the East Region and Bedfordshire County Coach. Always keen to develop his ideas, Paul has watched and worked with some of the best coaches in the world and shares the view of Butch Harmon (coach to Tiger Woods), that teaching golf is one of the best jobs in the world. Every day offers the thrill of helping golfers improve: 'It can be like watching your child ride their bike for the very first time'.

CHAPTER 1

Introduction

The definition of golf in a dictionary is: a game played on a large open course, the object of which is to hit a ball using clubs, with as few strokes as possible, into each of usually eighteen holes. If only it was as simple as that!

Many golfers struggle through their weekly round with the usual mixture of the good, the bad and the ugly. However hard they try, they can't progress past a certain point and even weekly visits to the practice range don't seem to bear fruit.

One round the driving is good and the iron shots are bad, the next round the iron shots improve but the driving goes off and when finally both are working well together, the putting is terrible. If this sounds like your golf, you are in the majority, but rest assured your game could improve. Whether your ambition is to score under a hundred or break par there are many ways to develop your golf skills; this book aims to guide you through a number of ideas that will help.

THE TRIANGLE OF SUCCESS

For any player to make progress, it will help if they can appreciate the wide variety of skills associated with golf. These include factors such as power, control, touch and feel, combined with patience, determination and emotional stability.

If a player can make a small improvement in each of these areas then their game will blossom. Conversely, practising one aspect in isolation will still leave a player vulnerable to being let down by other parts of their game. This book introduces the concept of the Triangle of Success and divides golf into three key areas:

- Long Game Skills;
- Short Game Skills;
- On-Course Skills.

Each of these areas has a dedicated chapter.

Chapter 3. Long Game Skills begins by explaining impact – the moment of truth. By

Fig 1 The Triangle of Success.

learning about impact, a player can see that whatever happens to the ball it was due to what the club was doing when it contacted the ball. The ball doesn't care about how many knuckles were showing on the left hand or whether or not the player kept their balance, but it does care about the angle of the clubface and the direction that the head is taking. The chapter goes on to explain that the movements of a golf swing are natural and similar to a simple throwing action. It deals with generating and delivering power and it helps the golfer learn about the value of an excellent start position. A variety of useful drills are suggested to help the golfer experience good movements; it also deals with common problems.

Chapter 4. Short Game Skills Around 50 per cent of shots are played from within 50yd of the hole. A golfer who can develop a good short game will be a match for anyone. The topics covered include putting, chipping, pitching and bunker shots, but for a player to simply possess good long and short game skills alone, will not be sufficient for them to reach their full potential as a golfer. They must learn how to repeat these shots on the course under a variety of different circumstances.

Chapter 5. On-Course Skills The chapter begins with a section called 'Think Like a Champion'. This covers mental skills and habits that are common to top players and explains how all players can think in this way. These skills are then combined with those of course management and are described by giving an example of two golfers playing a few holes on the course.

'The Triangle of Success' can help a player take control of their game by identifying what they need to do and showing them how to do it.

Stages of Learning
When any new skills are being developed, it is well worth understanding the various stages of learning. These are:

1. Unconscious incompetence. A player is doing something wrong in their game but they don't know what the problem is.
2. Conscious incompetence. They discover the cause of the problem but they still make the same mistake.
3. Conscious competence. They learn a new correction but have to think consciously to make it happen.
4. Unconscious competence. Having practised enough the player has grooved a new habit that has become automatic.

These stages of learning illustrate that to know what you are doing wrong is not enough. When a player discovers what he needs to do right he can then set about learning to do it.

Some players may be well advised not to take on the challenge of something like a swing adjustment. For instance, if they have played for a very long time with a fade they may be wise to accept that shape of shot and use it as foundation for their game. (Many leading players prefer a left to right shot and as Lee Trevino famously said: 'You can talk to a slice, but a hook don't listen'.)

However, they might take a look at other skills such as their pitching that can be improved in a short time and could set them up with many more single putt opportunities. Or working on a new pre-shot routine that could dramatically improve consistency.

Regardless of the standard of your golf, you can improve and as you do so, you will have a lot of enjoyment along the way.

A BRIEF HISTORY

The exact origins of golf are uncertain. Throughout history reference can be found to games involving stick and ball but the game, as we know it is generally seen to have evolved in Scotland, and as far back as 1457 golf was mentioned in a Scottish Act of Parliament. During this period King James II was concerned that archery practice was being ignored in favour of golf. As a result he considered it a threat to national security and declared that it should not be played. Fifty years elapsed before the ban was lifted and the game of golf resumed as a popular sport and pastime.

The first golf club came into existence in 1744. It was formed as the Gentlemen Golfers of Edinburgh, later to be called the Honourable Company of Edinburgh Golfers, and it was through this company that the first set of rules were drawn up. In 1754 the Royal and Ancient Club was established as the Society of St Andrews, in the Ancient Kingdom of Fife.

The earliest courses were built on land close to the sea and these became known as links courses. This land was often grazed by livestock, that kept the grass at a reasonable length, and featured many naturally occurring hazards such as sand-filled holes known as bunkers. In time, golf courses appeared at inland locations often near to railway lines for easy access and convenience.

Interest in golf has grown steadily over time, with improvements in equipment often encouraging periods of rapid growth. The 'guttie' ball, one of the earliest balls, made golf far less expensive and led to a dramatic increase in the number of golfers during the second half of the nineteenth century. While the introduction of the steel shaft in the 1920s promoted the game still further.

The past twenty years has seen a number of British and European tournament golfers achieving tremendous success on the world stage. This has created huge media interest and helped to spawn the most recent generation of golfer.

During the year 2000 golf participation in the UK was gauged at 3.8 million adults, aged fifteen and above. From this number 1.6 million are considered regular players inasmuch as they play at least once a month. (Figures courtesy of Sports Marketing Surveys Ltd.)

THE RULES AND SCORING

Golf is a game of great honour and tradition and in the absence of a referee or umpire, it is based on personal integrity. The rules of play are laid down by the Royal and Ancient Golf Club of St Andrews in Scotland and the United States Golf Association. Most players' knowledge of the rules evolve as they gain in experience, sometimes learning from their own mistakes. In the early stages of playing it is certainly not necessary to know every rule before setting foot on the course, however it is important to understand a few basics and in particular have a good appreciation of golf etiquette.

Scoring

The basis of the scoring game is par. Each hole on the course has its own par based mainly on its length, the par figure will be three for short holes, four for mid-length holes or five for the longest holes. The total par of the course is the aggregate of all eighteen holes and it is this figure that a golfer uses to evaluate his score.

Handicaps

There are many outstanding features about the game of golf, one of the most significant

Men	Par	Ladies
0–250	3	0–200
220–500	4	201–400
500+	5	400+

Fig 2 The distances in yards that help determine the par of a hole.

however being the system of handicapping that allows golfers of widely differing ability to compete with each other on level terms. A golf handicap will be administered by the player's golf club and once established, will fluctuate with their performance in organized competitions. The details of the system are fairly complicated but to help the newcomer grasp the basic concept, consider the following:

If over ten rounds of golf your average score was fifteen over par (that is, par for the course is seventy, your average score was eighty-five) then your handicap would be around fifteen. When your score is lower than the average outlined above then your handicap will be reduced, when however your score is higher it will be increased.

To establish an initial handicap each individual golfer is required to play three rounds, these have to be played with another player who records the score; this player must already hold an official handicap. In the UK the maximum handicap for men is twenty-eight and for ladies it is forty-five. Once accredited with their new handicap, a novice player can compete against any other golfer and have a genuine chance of beating them. As an added benefit, a handicap also acts as a golf passport that identifies an individual as a golfer and in most cases permits them to play any course. It would be very difficult to play football at Wembley, or tennis at Wimbledon, but a golfer could arrange a round of golf at St Andrews for the price of a daily green fee.

Scoring Systems

The two basic scoring systems are stroke play and match play. The majority of the big tournaments that appear on television are stroke play, although there are some notable exceptions such as the Ryder Cup that is a match play event.

Stroke Play

Stroke play involves completing every hole then adding the score from each of these holes together giving a gross total. The player then subtracts their handicap, leaving a net score that is compared to the total par for the course.

For example; Player A with a handicap of fifteen scores eighty on a course with a par of seventy – gross score 80, minus 15, net score 65, result 5 under par. Player B with a five handicap scores seventy-five in the same competition – gross score 75, minus 5, net score 70, result level par. Stroke play usually involves a large field of competitors with the lowest net score winning the first prize.

Match Play

Match play is a hole-by-hole competition between two individuals. Each hole is won, lost or halved. A player wins at match play when he has a holes up lead greater than the number of holes remaining, that is, two holes ahead with only one hole left. This result would be recorded as a victory by 2 and 1. Match play also takes account of the two players' handicaps although it does so using a different system from stroke play that works as follows:

before a match begins the two players compare handicaps. The higher handicap player is allowed extra strokes but these strokes are allocated on the way round rather than simply being deducted at the end of the game. The player cannot choose to use a stroke when he sees fit, instead they are assigned using the stroke index.

Each hole on the course has its own stroke index and this number is listed on the score-card. The lower the number, the more difficult the hole – for example: stroke index 1 is the most difficult, stroke index 6 is the sixth most difficult and stroke index 18 is the easiest.

If the players' handicaps are 5 and 15 the difference is 10 strokes which means the player with the higher handicap is allowed an extra stroke on holes with a stroke index of 10 and less. On these 'stroke holes' this player deducts one stroke from his score – i.e. gross 5, net 4. The lowest net score wins the hole.

The Scorecard

Every golf course has its own individual score card offering information on each hole. This includes hole number, hole length, par and stroke index as well as columns for the score. In official competition, cards are exchanged on the first tee so that nobody marks their own card. Using the appropriate player and marker columns, scores are noted and on completion of the round the cards are cross-referenced and signed by both parties.

Etiquette

Golf etiquette can be described as consideration of two things; other players and the course.

Considering Other Players

- Safety; Do not play until the players ahead are out of range. Shout 'fore' if you hit a ball towards another player. If you hear a shout directed towards you, don't look up to see where it is coming from, instead make yourself as small as you can.
- Speed of play; Avoid slow play. Be ready when it is your turn to play and do so without undue delay. Keep up with the group in front and not just ahead of the group behind. If you cannot keep up then stand to the side and allow the group behind to pass and continue when they are a safe distance ahead.
- Noise and distractions; Golf is essentially a quiet game, when someone is playing a shot remain silent and in a position that is not interfering in any way. Also be aware of other players on adjacent holes who may be within earshot.
- Show compassion and play in good humour. Golf can be tough at times so be respectful to other players who may be struggling and if you are having a bad round, don't let your mood spoil the enjoyment of your partners.

Consideration for the Course

- Replace divots.
- Repair pitch marks from balls landing on the green.
- Rake footprints in bunkers.
- Avoid taking bags and trolleys onto tees and greens.
- Walk carefully on the greens and be sure not to drag your feet especially in the area close to the hole.

Basic Rules

Play the Ball as it Lies

In general, you can only advance the ball by hitting it with the club. Once on the green the

---

Etiquette and the Beginner

When you are playing your first few games of golf other players won't be concerned about your score or how you apply the rules, but they will be concerned if you play too slowly, fail to repair damage or ignore common safety advice. If you show good golf etiquette you have nothing to fear.

INTRODUCTION

Comp _____

Date _____

Player A _____ Handicap _____ Allowance _____

Player B _____ Handicap _____ Allowance _____

SSS		
White/70		
Yellow/69		

Marker	Hole	White	Yellow	Par	S.I.	Player A	Player B	Points
	1	503	486	5	6			
	2	357	341	4	10			
	3	133	110	3	16			
	4	393	384	4	2			
	5	147	139	3	18			
	6	280	266	4	12			
	7	173	163	3	14			
	8	362	343	4	4			
	9	331	316	4	8			
	Out	2679	2548	34				
	10	447	433	4	3			
	11	427	414	4	5			
	12	358	342	4	9			
	13	154	130	3	17			
	14	416	392	4	1			
	15	493	470	5	7			
	16	168	150	3	15			
	17	481	476	5	11			
	18	332	314	4	13			
	In	3276	3121	36				
	Out	2679	2548	34				
	Total	5955	5669	70				

Handicap

Nett Score

Marker Sign _____

Player Sign _____

Result _____

Fig 3 A golf scorecard.

10

ball may be marked and lifted, but mostly it is played as it is found. Every time the ball is struck it counts as one stroke; in addition an 'air shot' also counts as one.

Order of Play

On the first tee the order of play is determined by the draw sheet in competition or the toss of a coin in friendly play. Subsequently the order is determined by the score from the previous hole, the golfer with the lowest score tees off first, second best score tees off second and so on. The player who tees off first is said to have the honour. If the scores were tied then the order is carried over from the previous tee. Once in play, the person furthest from the hole plays first.

The Teeing Ground

A pair of markers identifies the teeing ground. The ball must be played from this teeing ground but not forward of an imaginary straight line between the markers. The permitted area extends back to a depth of two club lengths. A player may stand outside the teeing ground so long as the ball is inside.

The Putting Green

When your ball is on the green there are some special rules that apply. As already mentioned you can mark, and pick up your ball. This may be necessary for cleaning purposes or because it is on the line of a fellow competitor's putt. When putting on the green, the flagstick must be taken out or attended. If you leave it in any ball striking the stick incurs a two-shot penalty. When playing from off the green this penalty does not apply, so leave the flag in and use it as a backstop. You are allowed to repair pitch marks that may be on the line of your shot, but you cannot repair spike marks, so out of courtesy to other players walk carefully on the greens.

Lost Ball

When a ball cannot be found it is defined as lost. This incurs a penalty shot and requires that the shot be replayed from its original position. This is known as 'stroke and distance', that is, if a tee shot is lost the player has to play another shot from the tee that counts as his third shot. Under no circumstances can a player drop a ball in the area in which he considers the ball lost.

If a player hits a shot that he believes is in trouble and may be lost, to assist the speed of play, a golfer may hit another shot from his existing position, which is called a provisional ball. If the original ball is found, he can pick up the provisional without penalty, if the original is lost then he must complete the hole using the provisional ball; the penalty is still stroke and distance. For example if a tee shot is lost, the provisional ball counts as the third shot, the next shot hit with the provisional counts as the fourth shot. The purpose of the provisional ball is to spare the player from having a long walk back to the site of the original shot.

Hazards

All golf courses are guarded by hazards, these include lakes, ponds, ditches and bunkers. When a ball lies in a hazard you are allowed to play a shot but the club is not permitted to touch the surface of the ground or water until the downswing.

Yellow stakes define a water hazard and if your ball finishes in one of these areas you have three options:

1. Play your ball as it lies, no penalty.
2. Drop a ball behind the hazard keeping the point where the ball crossed the hazard in a line between you and the hole, you may retreat as far back as you wish. This incurs a one-stroke penalty.

3. Replay from the position of the original shot. This also incurs a one-stroke penalty.

Red stakes define a lateral water hazard. These generally run alongside rather than across a hole and allow the same choices as the regular water hazard plus two additional ones:

1. Drop a ball within two club lengths of the point that the ball last crossed the hazard, but not nearer to the hole.
2. Drop a ball within two club lengths on the opposite side or bank of the hazard at a point equidistant from the hole.

Unplayable Lies
During the course of a round it is possible that you may find your ball in a position such that you cannot hit it, for example, under a bush. In this situation you can declare the ball unplayable and for a penalty of one shot choose one of the following options:

1. Drop a ball within two club lengths of the point where the ball lies, but not nearer the hole.
2. Drop a ball directly behind the point where the ball lies, extending as far back as you wish, but keeping the original

point in a straight line between you and the hole.
3. Replay from the position of the original shot.

Relief Situations
Occasionally your ball may lie in an area that entitles you to a free drop. These areas include man-made obstructions, rabbit scrapes and standing water left after heavy rain. In these situations establish the nearest point that offers full relief and is not nearer to the hole and then drop within one club length of this point without penalty.

How to Take a Drop

When taking a drop stand erect, hold the ball at shoulder height and let it drop. If you are dropping on a slope and the ball rolls back into the hazard you must redrop. If it happens again then place the ball at the point it first hit the ground.

Summary
The rules outlined here will give you an excellent start point, but do yourself a favour – get a copy of the Rules of Golf and keep it in your bag.

CHAPTER 2

Equipment

THE EVOLUTION OF CLUB DESIGN

As the game of golf has evolved so has the need to improve and develop equipment. Originally a set of clubs was made up of all wooden-headed clubs including a wooden putter. Shafts were originally made from thick and heavy branches of hazelwood, these were followed by ash and later by hickory. Heads were shaped from apple or beechwood although neither proved as strong as the persimmon that replaced them.

The first crafted clubs had the shafts spliced to the heads, which were long-nosed and with shallow club faces. The shafts were particularly whippy and so the playing characteristics made it difficult to combine both clubhead speed and accuracy. All shots tended to be swept cleanly off the ground which necessitated the introduction of some thin-bladed iron clubs so that difficult lies could be dealt with more easily. These early hand-forged irons had no grooves on the face, but still enabled the ball to get airborne. Eventually they were replaced by the next generation of drop-forged irons featuring grooves that imparted more spin to the ball and improved the flight considerably.

There was little change in club design until the 1960s when Karsten Solheim designed the first cavity back irons and putters using the investment casting technique to produce the heads. The cavity back design featured more weight around the perimeter of the head that, in turn, expanded the effective hitting area and thus increased the margin for error. From that point on bladed irons have become far less popular, although a few players still prefer the special feel and feedback offered by a blade. The very latest designs are able to offer the best of both feel and forgiveness as developments in technology continue.

As wooden clubs evolved, heads became deeper and more rounded and were fitted with face inserts to offer protection from the newer balls that were becoming harder. Brass or steel sole plates were also fitted to protect the underside of the club. This innovation had the effect of lowering the centre of gravity thus enabling players to hit higher shots.

Possibly the most significant change in wood design occurred in the 1980s when the metal head was introduced. The clubheads were hollow and therefore had the weight around the outside; this had a similar effect to the cavity back iron, making them much more forgiving when shots are struck off-centre. This design allows players to get the ball airborne more easily and reduces sidespin, so hooks and slices are less severe. The introduction of titanium that is much stronger and lighter than steel, has allowed heads to grow larger without becoming too heavy. These 'oversize' clubs offer even bigger effective hitting areas and therefore better performance.

The other main component of a golf club is the shaft. The move from hickory to steel in the 1920s and 30s had probably a greater effect on the game than any other single advance. Steel had far less torque or twist in the shaft and allowed players to hit the ball harder and still maintain control. Golf administrators, however, feared that players would hit the ball much further and they did.

The more recent innovation in shaft design has seen the introduction of graphite. This is much lighter than steel and allows the manufacturer to locate more weight in the head without disturbing the overall balance of the club. Graphite shafts also absorb the vibration that is experienced on a mishit shot. For those players who suffer wrist, elbow or shoulder injuries this is a tremendous advantage.

The evolution of equipment through technology has allowed the top players to hit the ball further and straighter than ever before. It has also helped the average player who can now derive more pleasure and satisfaction and as such has helped the growth of the game.

THE COMPOSITION OF A SET

The Rules of Golf allow a maximum of fourteen clubs. The standard set combination is three woods, nine irons and a putter, leaving room for a speciality club such as a seven wood or lob wedge. Each club has its own unique combination of length and loft thus a player can produce a wide range of distances without needing to change their swing.
The longer shafted clubs have less loft and therefore hit lower, longer shots. Fig 5 illus-

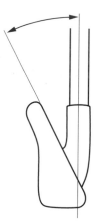

Fig 4 How loft is measured.

trates club length changing by half an inch per club and loft changing by 3–5 degrees. In playing terms this results in a distance differential of 10–15yd per club. In practice the contents of a player's bag tend to vary depending on his style and indeed standard of play.

	Length (inches)	Loft (degrees)
Woods		
Driver	43+	8–12
3	42	13–16
5	41	19–21
7	40	23–27
Irons		
1	39.5	15
2	39	18
3	38.5	21
4	38	24
5	37.5	28
6	37	32
7	36.5	36
8	36	40
9	35.5	45
Pitching Wedge	32	50
Sand Iron	35	55
Lob Wedge	35	60

Specifications do vary between manufacturers.

Fig 5 Length and loft measurements for a set of men's clubs.

What is Loft?

The loft of a club refers to the angle of the face and its influence on the trajectory of a shot. It is measured as the difference between the angle of the face and the shaft.

The Beginner

A small collection of clubs is recommended allowing the beginner to discover the differences between clubs and therefore learning their 'job description'. For instance a combination of 3 wood, 7 iron and sand iron would give a clearly defined result for each club. As the player develops consistency they can add in to fill the gaps. An excellent combination for the first few months of play is: 3 wood. 3, 5, 7, 9, Sand Iron and Putter, this is known as a half set.

The High-Handicapper

This player will frequently benefit by avoiding a driver, instead teeing off with a 3 wood thus gaining control and improved consistency. On long fairway shots they may also prefer to use lofted woods in preference to long irons. This player's bag may look like this:

3, 5 and 7 wood. 4, 5, 6, 7, 8, 9, PW, SW and Putter.

The Mid-Handicap Player

This player will usually be able to use a driver for tee shots although low lofts should be avoided. They will also appreciate the value of the short game and may have an extra wedge.

Driver, 3 and 5 wood. 3, 4, 5, 6, 7, 8, 9, PW, SW, Lob Wedge and Putter.

The Low-Handicap Player

The expert player will often have the required power to use long irons and may prefer them to lofted woods; he would also carry an extra wedge for extra control in the short game.

Driver and 3 wood. 2, 3, 4, 5, 6, 7, 8, 9, PW, SW, Lob Wedge and Putter.

The Tournament Professional

A professional will often have a pool of clubs far greater in number than the maximum of fourteen. From this selection he will choose the set make-up that will suit the type of course he is playing on any particular week. For instance, playing on a very tight course he may take a one iron to use on specific tee shots or on a long course he may favour an extra fairway wood.

Did You Know?

Travelling workshops from the leading club manufacturers support the major professional tours. These excellent facilities enable players to adjust the specifications of their clubs to suit the prevailing conditions.

For example, in windy conditions a lower trajectory on iron shots may be an advantage. This can be achieved by either changing the loft of each club or by strategically adding lead weighting strips to the back of the clubhead.

CLUB FITTING

To maximize your game, correctly fitted clubs are essential. All golfers are individuals and as such the standard or average specification will not suit all. There are several key features that can be adjusted to match you and your swing:

1. Head design
2. Length
3. Lie angle
4. Shaft type and flex
5. Grip Size

Head Design

The majority of irons are either cast or forged. These terms relate to their style of manufacture; the cast club is made in a mould and

Fig 6 A good combination of clubs for the new player.

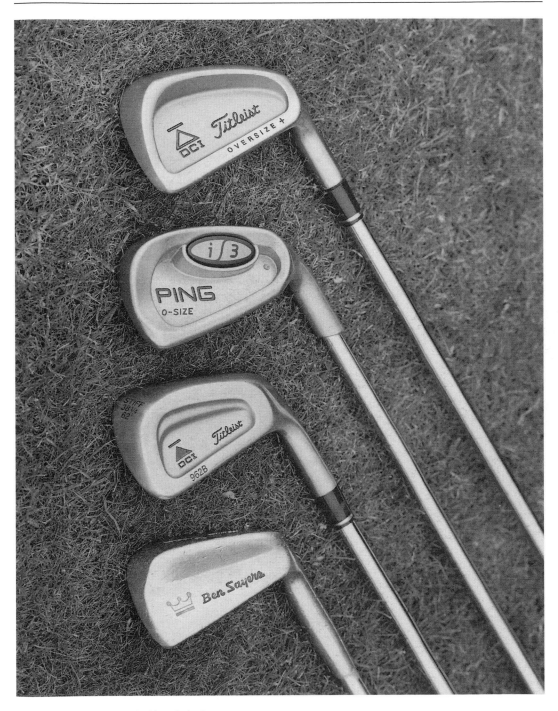

Fig 7 A selection of clubhead designs.

typically has a perimeter weighted style, the forged club (often known as a blade) is hammered into shape and features most of its weight in the centre of the head.

Both styles of club perform well when hit in the centre or sweet spot, however, slight mishits are punished less by the cast club's perimeter weighting and as such it is generally seen as more forgiving for most players. The expert player who strikes the ball with great accuracy may choose the forged club for its softer feel from the head, although this similar feel is now available in cast club design through heat treatments and shaft inserts that filter vibration.

Length

Club length has a great influence on setting up the shot, too long and posture is too vertical, too short and players tend to bend forward too much. Length also affects consistency of striking – a longer shaft is more powerful, but more difficult to control and may create mishits. Research has shown that for every half-inch you hit off-centre you lose around 5 per cent in distance. 'Proper club length allows you the opportunity to consistently hit the ball solidly.' (Titleist, leading golf equipment company).

A player's height is the start point to assess the correct club length.

Height	Length
5ft 2in–5ft 4in	–½in
5ft 4in–5ft 7in	–¼in
5ft 7in–6ft 1in	0
6ft 1in–6ft 4in	+½in
6ft 4in–6ft 7in	+1in
6ft 7in–6ft 9in	+1½in

Fig 8 Suggested guidelines for club length, based on men's specifications.

Lie Angle

This is measured from the centre line of the shaft to the ground when the club is soled correctly.

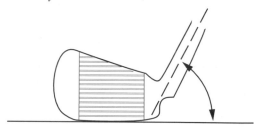

Fig 9 How the lie angle is measured.

This lie angle needs to be considered in two ways.

- Lie angle at address;
- Lie angle at impact.

Of these the impact position is of most value because it takes account of the swing and the way the shaft bends as a result of the forces in the swing. Lie angle influences shot direction:

- too upright – the clubface is angled left and the heel may well drag on the ground causing the face to close and hit left;
- too flat – the clubface is angled right and the toe may drag; open the face and hit right.

'An improper lie angle at impact will adversely affect the flight of the ball' (Ping Golf, a specialist manufacturer of custom fit clubs).

The correct lie angle is established by applying tape to the sole of a club and hitting from a board that leaves a mark indicating the angle of the club at impact. This is then fine-tuned until the correct angle is found.

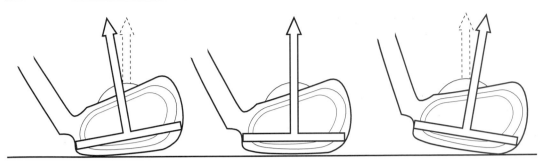

Fig 10 How the lie angle affects shot direction.

Shaft Type and Flex

Shaft choice influences trajectory, distance and feel from the shot. Most clubs feature either steel or graphite shafts. Each has its own merits. Graphite is lighter allowing a heavier head weight that may add extra power. In addition, graphite absorbs vibration from mishits. Steel has less torque or twist possibly offering more control and gives more feed back about the quality of contact.

Fig 11 Impact tape used to establish the correct lie angle.

5 Iron Distance (Yards)	100–120	120–140	140–160	160–180	180–200
Shaft Flex	L	A	R	S	X
	Ladies' Flex	A-Flex	Men's Regular Flex	Men's Stiff Flex	Men's Extra Stiff Flex

Fig 12 Recommended shaft flex based on the distance of a five iron.

Shaft flex needs to match the speed of the player's swing. A slower swing will suit a more flexible shaft, a more powerful swing requires a stiffer shaft. The following chart gives a good start point.

Grip Size

Finding the correct grip size has a direct bearing on the hand action that occurs in your swing, this can influence both power and direction. Grips that are too large prevent a powerful release of the club, while a small grip creates overactive hands that may result in a shot hooking to the left. For an excellent fit the two middle fingers of the left hand should just touch the heel of the palm. If there's a large gap, your grips are too big and if your fingers are digging in, they are too small.

THE GOLF BALL

Evolution

The earliest reference to golf balls is found in 1554, and it is thought that golfers first played with a wooden ball that was then followed by one with a leather cover and probably stuffed with animal hair. The most successful balls however, were stuffed with wet goose feathers that expanded on drying, and were hand-made by specialist ball makers. It was said to take a top hat full of feathers to fill each ball. Due to the time taken to make them, these feathery balls were very expensive, the cost of one ball being roughly equivalent to a man's average weekly wage. Also, they were not very hard-wearing and soon became misshapen.

Despite these shortcomings, it was not until 1850 that this ball was superseded by one made from gutta-percha. The 'guttie' was a solid ball that felt harder, and was more lively and durable. It was mass-produced and consequently far less expensive; this made golf affordable and the game took off. During the development of the 'guttie' it was discovered that a perfectly smooth ball didn't fly well and that worn balls with scuffs and scratches performed better. As we now know, it is an aerodynamic necessity to have an irregular surface to produce the right flight, so the forerunner to the modern dimple was born. Various patterns on the surface were tested including an imitation of the old feather balls' stitched seam.

In 1899 the Haskell ball was patented. This was a three-piece ball; a core with a rubber thread wound around it and a moulded cover made from gutta-percha. The improved performance was dramatic – it delivered less of a shock when mishit, flew higher and most importantly went 30yd further. The 'guttie' was obsolete by 1904. Not long afterwards it was discovered that balata, a gum from the bully-tree in South America, improved the feel of the clubface still further, so it replaced gutta-percha as a cover material. In recent years three-piece wound balls with a balata cover have proved less popular due to the cost of manufacture and the development of the more durable two-piece ball.

Which Ball?

Today's choice of ball is tremendously varied. To decide what you are looking for from your golf ball, two of the main features to consider are feel (hard or soft), and spin rate.

The following guidelines are a generalization but may give you a start point.

Beginner/ High-Handicap Player
Opt for a two-piece ball with low spin for maximum distance and durability. This ball will feel hard and lively at impact, and the low spin rate will minimize hooking and slicing.

Mid-Handicap Player
Choose a medium spin ball with a durable cover for a blend of distance and control. This may be either a two or three-piece design, that combines the latest technology to give a bit of everything.

Low-Handicap Player
Choose a ball with a high spin rate and a soft cover for control and manoeuvrability. This ball will feel soft at impact and stop quickly on the green.

Experiment with balls, but when you find a model that you really enjoy, try to stick with it, as your game will benefit from having one less variable.

CHAPTER 3

Long Game Skills

Long game skills are the first element in the 'Triangle of Success'.

Fig 13 The Triangle of Success.

IMPACT – THE MOMENT OF TRUTH!

Golf is an individual game, played by individual characters using individual swings. Amongst the best players in the world there is a wide variety of swings, however the common denominator is a good impact position. Please note this does not mean that each has the same impact position, but it does mean that each good player knows his impact position and, most importantly, is able to repeat that position and produce consistent shots.

'The point is that it doesn't matter if you look like a beast before or after the hit, as long as you look like a beauty at the moment of impact' (Seve Ballesteros, winner of five Major Championships).

Contact to Loft the Ball

If you have watched golf on television you will have noticed how many top golfers playing an iron shot take a divot (a piece of turf removed when playing a shot). When beginners or high-handicap players take a divot they mostly hit a poor shot. Why is this? The answer lies in where the bottom of the swing actually occurs. The beginner will often try to lift the ball into the air by attempting an upward hit. This involves the low point of the swing arriving before the ball and rising at impact. In this scenario if the swing touches the ground, then a divot will occur before the ball causing poor contact and loss of power. If this swing doesn't touch the ground it may well begin to rise too quickly and contact the ball above its equator producing a 'topped' shot. When this happens the player is likely to try even harder to hit up at the ball thereby making the problem worse so beginning a vicious circle of compounding the errors.

The expert player uses a swing that reaches its low point right at the ball or a little past it, so that any divot is taken after impact. Therefore the ball is lofted by the loft of the clubface and not lifted by the swing. When playing a shot from a tee using a wood, the ball can be struck with a slightly upward swing that is achieved by a simple adjustment to the position of the ball in relation to the feet rather than attempting to lift the shot.

Contact for Direction

Why Does a Golf Ball Curve?
When a golf ball is lofted, once in flight it can do only one of three things:

- fly straight in the direction it has been sent;
- curve to the right;
- curve to the left.

The flight that occurs is determined by the angle of the clubface at impact, the moment of truth. The ball responds only to that position and knows nothing of any other position that may have been achieved in the swing. When the face is aimed to the right of its path at impact, sidespin is imparted and the ball will curve to the right. This is known as open. When the face is aimed to the left of its path at impact, sidespin is again imparted and the ball curves to the left. This is known as closed. When the clubface points or aims in the direction of its path, then the ball will fly straight with no sidespin and therefore no curve. This position is known as square. The golfer's grip is the feature that most influences the clubface angle.

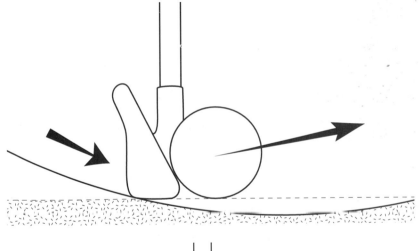

Fig 14a An iron struck with a descending blow produces a divot past the ball.

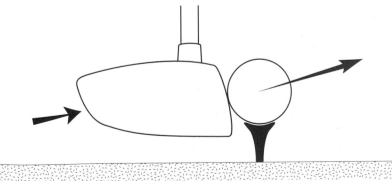

Fig 14b A wood played from a tee struck on the upswing with no divot.

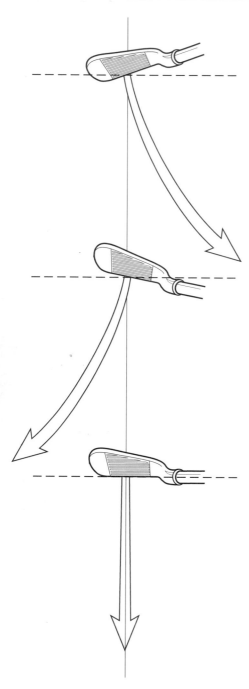

Fig 15 How the angle of the clubface at impact influences the curve on the shot.

Sidespin and the Effect of Loft

The choice of club influences the amount of curve on the shot. A short iron imparts considerable backspin so reducing the amount of sidespin; a driver with very little loft may produce more sidespin and therefore a shot with more curve.

This relationship between clubface loft and sidespin is good reason to choose a driver that has more rather than less loft, that is, 11-degree rather than 8-degree.

Why Does a Golf Ball Not Start Straight?
When a golf ball leaves the clubface it can do only one of three things:

- set out on target;
- set out to the right of target;
- set out to the left of target.

This starting direction is influenced by the clubhead's path at impact. When the path of the clubhead is swinging across to the right it is known as an in to out swing and will tend to start the ball to the right. When the path is swinging to the left it is known as an out to in swing and will tend to start the ball to the left.

Many golfers find the terms 'in to out' and 'out to in' confusing. As an alternative *see* Fig 17 below and relate the swing to the colour that it passes through on either side of the ball. A grey to grey swing would start the ball left of target (out to in). While a black to black swing would start the ball right of target (in to out).

Moment of Impact

The moment of impact has a duration of half a millisecond (0.0005 sec); that means a golfer playing eighteen holes with an average score is hitting the ball for less than one-tenth of a second!

Fig 16a An in to out swing path.

Fig 16b An out to in swing path.

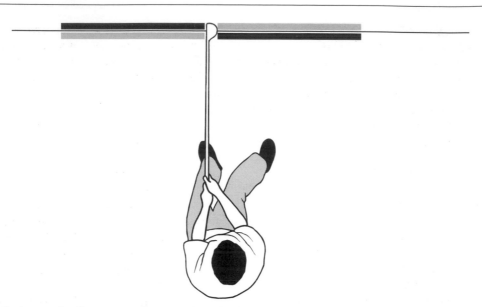

Fig 17 Swing path. Grey to grey is out to in. Black to black is in to out.

When a golfer plays a shot he is standing to the side of the ball and must swing in an arc at an inclined angle so the club should be swung inside on the backswing, onto the target line at impact and then back inside on the followthrough. This swing path will start the ball on target. The player's body and in particular shoulder alignment are key influences in the swing path.

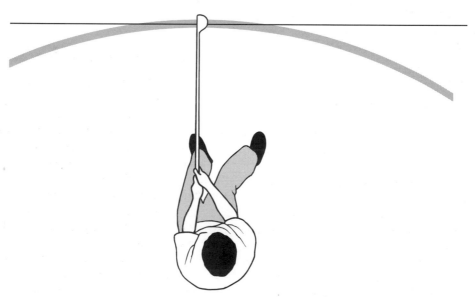

Fig 18 A swing path that is in to in.

Having established that the player stands to the side of the ball it is also important to note that the ball sits on the ground. This requires the body to bend forward. This body angle or posture influences the angle of attack onto the ball. Too much bend creates a steep angle of attack that approaches the ball with a vertical or chopping style. This may be functional on short iron shots, but will not work well with long irons or woods.

A posture that is too upright tends to cause the swing angle to be more horizontal or shallow and will reach its low point too early so the club will be rising as it meets the ball, often causing topped shots. This style of swing generally works better when hitting from a tee as it creates a slightly upward angle of attack.

The swing path and angle of attack work very closely together. A player who develops an out to in swing has a steep angle of attack and will feel most confident with short irons. Equally, a player with an in to out swing has a shallow angle of attack and will usually favour wood shots.

To sum up, the swing path influences the start direction of the shot and the face angle produces the curve and therefore finishing position of the shot.

THE SWING

As mentioned in the previous chapter golf is an individual game. To allow the individual to prosper it is worth recognising that the golf swing shares a similar look and feel to many other activities. For example a side arm throw and a baseball swing both involve a side on action that many people find both comfortable and natural. Each of these combines a turn of the body with a co-ordinated swing of the arm(s).

Making this association is very valuable. Many players, especially in the early stages, try too hard to find perfect swing positions at the expense of a free flowing swing. Clearly there will be varying degrees of natural ability but to find what is natural and then develop it, is preferable to being placed into statue-like positions that may appear correct but have no flow.

Practice Drills to Find or Free up Your Natural Swing

- Eyes closed drill. Without using a ball, take a stance hovering the club six inches above the ground, close your eyes and make five practice swings. Enjoy your swing like never before, feel the co-ordination of arms and body – when the eyes are open, sight dominates the senses so touch and feel are reduced.
- Walk-through drill. Tee up five balls in a row, approximately 6in apart. Walk through the line of balls hitting one after another without stopping. Feel the momentum of the club as it flows back and forth. Repeat five times and then take the same freedom of swing into a regular shot.

Maximize Your Natural Ability

Having said that the swing is a natural movement, it is also fair to say that playing golf to a reasonable standard requires the player to develop considerable power and control. Research has shown that golfers can generate clubhead speed of over 100mph and that the force applied to the ball at impact is nearly a ton. Scientists have been able to establish that a good golfer can generate up to 4hp of energy which in turn requires at least 30lb of muscle to produce it.

From this information it can be concluded that the large muscles of the body, and not just the arms, are essential in developing a powerful swing.

Fig 19a, b (ABOVE AND ABOVE RIGHT)
A side arm throw shares many features
with a golf swing.

Fig 19c.

Fig 20 The walk-through drill.

When Tiger Woods hits a drive that carries 300yd, he achieves a clubhead speed of around 120mph.

Generating Power

To engage these large muscles of the body the golfer needs to coil them to create a torsion effect. During the backswing, the shoulders need to turn more than the hips so the large muscles of the back, hips and thighs are stretched. The legs play an important role as they provide stability for the whole process. On the downswing, the power is uncoiled producing clubhead speed.

Many players try hard to turn everything during their backswing but lose power because they have no resistance. To help understand resistance, imagine looking down on a player from above, i.e. a bird's eye view. A good swing, observed from this position, would show a shoulder turn of 90 degrees, a hip turn of 45 degrees and a knee turn of around 25 degrees. To simplify, the knees make a quarter turn, the hips a half turn and the shoulders a full turn (*see* Fig 21). This ratio will vary from player to player and will be influenced by their age and flexibility but, appreciate the concept of coil and resistance and you will maximize your power.

Another way to understand resistance is to imagine hitting a golf ball standing on ice, wearing street shoes. A short swing with little power might be fine but a full swing would be impossible because there would be no traction from the ground and no resistance.

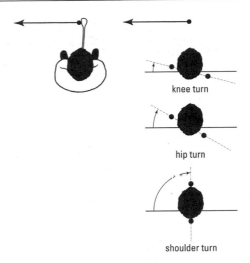

Fig 21 The body coil from above.

knee turn

hip turn

shoulder turn

Delivering Power

A coiled backswing has potential power. To deliver actual power requires the uncoiling action to follow the correct sequence. This sequence is present in the natural throwing action mentioned earlier. It involves the lower body shifting to the left as the lead hip turns towards the target. The arms then deliver the 'hit'. This may sound complicated, if so, simply practise making a side arm throw and feel the sequence of events.

Power Loss

Some players are so eager to hit the ball they begin to swing down with their arms before the hips. This causes a serious power loss.

Practice Drills for Power

- Cross your arms over your chest and adopt a golf posture (keeping a straight spine, bend from the hips and then flex the knees). Retaining the bend in the right knee, make a backswing and feel resistance

A Key for Good Resistance

During the backswing an excellent swing thought is to keep the right knee bent, and above or inside the ankle. When the knee straightens or moves outwards resistance is lost.

Fig 22 A drill to feel a powerful body coil.

from the ground up. The correct action will allow your body weight to shift to the inside of the right foot, as it would in a side arm throw. Your head may move a couple of inches to the right, but not lift up. Then feel the change of direction, lead with the lower body and turn through to a finish with your weight above the left foot.

- To emphasize the coil, adopt a similar position but allow the left arm to hang down and take hold of your left shoulder. Then make a backswing and again feel how the power muscles are engaged.

Try both of these drills in front of a mirror for improved feedback.

Adding the Club

Developing power in the large muscles is crucial, but the club has to strike the ball in the correct position. As already mentioned in connection with the impact position, the angle of the clubface and the direction and steepness of the swingpath create the resultant shot. The contact point on the face will also have a significant effect on the flight, distance and direction of the ball. Consequently, the hands and arms attached to the club are crucial factors in achieving the desired result.

In fact the turning action of the body tends to take the club around (horizontal) and the arm swing tends to lift the club up (vertical), so combining both parts is the key to a good swing. If either one dominates, the shot will suffer. Using simple checkpoints is a great way to achieve this blend.

Club Positions

Whenever the shaft is parallel to the ground, it should be parallel to the ball to target line.

Fig 23 A second drill to feel body coil.

This applies at waist-high on the backswing, the top of the backswing, waist-high on the downswing and waist-high on the follow-through.

Definition of Ball to Target Line

An imaginary straight line running from the ball to the target and from the ball away from the target. This line will be referred to a number of times and it will help to have a clear image.

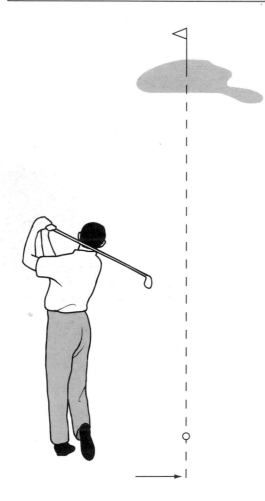

Fig 24 The ball to target line.

Waist-high on the Backswing
The move that initiates the swing is known as the takeaway. A sound takeaway will involve moving the club, arms and shoulders together. If this has been successful then the shaft will be parallel to the ball to target line when it is parallel to the ground.

Practising the Checkpoints

In practice, lay clubs down on the ground to help find the checkpoints for your swing.

If the lifting action of the arms has dominated, the shaft when parallel to the ground will be pointing left of target.

If the turning action of the body has dominated, the shaft when parallel to the ground will be pointing right of target.

At this point in the swing the clubface angle is also worth noting. This should be positioned so that the toe end is pointing skywards.

Top of the Backswing
As the backswing continues the arms will swing up as the body turns. Resistance from the lower half of the body will strongly influence the length of swing, but the conventional position will have the clubshaft somewhere near parallel to the ground. It is at this point that the shaft should again be parallel to the ball to target line.

The club will be above the right shoulder, the left arm comfortably straight and most of the body weight over the right foot.

Waist-high on the Downswing
This position is largely created by the movements that have initiated the downswing. To find the correct position requires the body to uncoil, leading with the hips, rather than swinging the arms and throwing the club out and away. When the shaft is parallel to the ground it should be parallel to the ball to target line.

Fig 25 (LEFT
AND BELOW)
*The first
checkpoint.*

Head Position

During the backswing there is no need to keep
your head perfectly still, as this will prevent your
weight from shifting to the right. An excellent
way to check this would involve watching your
shadow on the ground in front of you. Position
the shadow of your head over an old divot and
make a backswing – you should just reveal the
divot to sunlight.

Fig 26 (LEFT AND BELOW) The top of the swing.

A Common Problem for the Medium to Low Handicapper

A problem that can develop for the good player stems from an in to out swing. They may be hitting to the right and conclude they are slicing. They decide that they must be swinging out to in and embark upon a practice regime to 'correct' this by swinging even more in to out. Unfortunately, the harder they work at this the more the ball starts to the right.

If this sounds familiar check your divot line. It should be pointing on target or slightly left, but not to the right. The solution would be to feel your arms swing down before the body uncoils. It may feel as if you are swinging over the top of the ball, but it is only when the ball starts left of target that you will have over-cooked it.

Fig 27 (LEFT AND BELOW) Waist-high on the downswing.

If the arms have been thrown out, the shaft, when parallel to the ground will be pointing left of target and be delivered with an out to in path. As mentioned earlier, this creates a chopping action that tends to start the ball to the left. This type of swing may be successful with short irons but would struggle to hit woods accurately.

If the body has turned too much and left the arms behind, the shaft, when parallel to the ground will be pointing right of target and have an in to out path. This tends to start the ball to the right and has a very shallow angle of attack; this swing prefers the ball on a tee and therefore produces better results with woods rather than irons.

35

Fig 28 (LEFT AND BELOW) *Impact.*

Impact – the Moment of Truth

If the positions already mentioned have been achieved then impact will take care of itself. The hips will be leading the shoulders and be open to the target. The shoulders will be parallel to the target and the body weight favouring the left foot. From the face-on view, the shaft has caught up with the left arm and forms a straight line. The shaft must not lag behind or pass the left arm before impact.

Impact

Golfing great Henry Cotton used to teach his pupils to practise by hitting an old car tyre. This would enhance feel for impact and build up strength at the same time. A tyre can produce a large shock and possible injury so using an old cushion or heavy pillow may be easier.

Please note. This drill promotes good impact and should not restrict a good followthrough.

Fig 29 (LEFT AND BELOW). Waist-high on the followthrough.

Waist-high on the Followthrough
The body is continuing to turn, the weight is mostly on the left foot and again the clubshaft, when parallel to the ground, should be parallel to the ball to target line. This position in the swing illustrates the release action. The right arm has crossed or moved above the left and the toe end of the clubface is pointing skyward.

Release the Club

To feel the release, take a club and make some baseball swings. As the arms swing they naturally cross. If the left arm remains on top in the followthrough it will cause a slice.

The Finish Position
A good swing is finished with a good followthrough. The body will have turned so that the hips are towards the target and the

Fig 30 (LEFT AND BELOW). The finish position.

chest points left of target. The hands will be above the left shoulder and the clubshaft angled across the back of the neck. The left leg will have straightened as it receives the full shift of body weight. This 'posting up' also helps the turning action of the hips; if the left knee buckles then the hips tend to slide rather than turn. With balance intact the expert player is able to hold his position watching the ball in flight.

'The good player swings through the ball while the awkward player swings at it' (Ken Venturi).

Swing Summary

Reading through a whole list of swing details can fill your head with too much information. In reality you are probably achieving or getting close enough to many of the positions required. Remember much of the swing can be compared to the natural side-arm throwing action already mentioned. However, by appreciating good positions in the swing you will be able to develop your instinct to its full potential.

To achieve this you need to have a good concept of what the swing should be, and then work patiently to develop one part at a time. It is very difficult to hit a golf shot with more than one swing thought, and impossible to hit it with more than two.

Fortunately, there are several positions that influence the swing even before it begins. The address, set-up or start position.

THE S

The start position predetermines much of what will happen in your swing. It requires no great athletic ability although it does require some care and attention. Many players are happy to take a comfortable stance even though it may be incorrect, sadly this will compromise the performance of the swing.

To help remember the components of the start position think GASP Grip, Aim, Stance and Posture.

Rest assured, any changes in position become comfortable with repetition.

The Grip

The grip has a direct effect on the angle of the clubface and therefore on direction. As Gary Player, winner of the nine major championships has said: 'Without a proper grip no player can expect to hit accurate shots with even a fair degree of consistency.'

The Left Hand

- The handle should rest along the base of the fingers so that when you close your

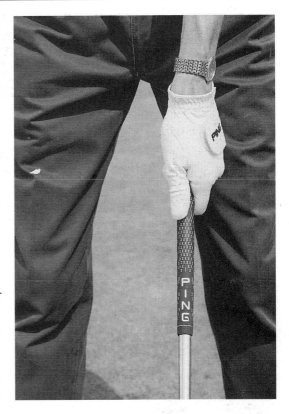

Fig 31a The left-hand grip.

hand the fleshy heel pad anchors the club securely in place.
- Now place your left thumb slightly to the right of centre, as you do this keep the joints of thumb and forefinger close together. Looking down, the player should be able to see two or three knuckles on the back of the hand or read the logo on their glove.

The Right Hand

- Introduce the right hand by wrapping the fingertips under the handle and close the hand over the left thumb.
- The right thumb should be just to the left of centre.

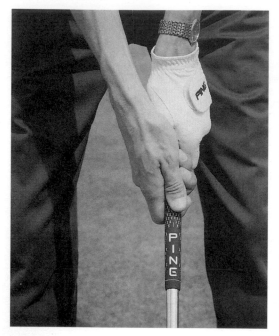

Fig 31b joined by the right hand.

Fig 32a The overlap or Vardon grip.

Overlap or Interlock

Linking the hands is an area of confusion. Many players get so concerned about whether to overlap or interlock that they miss the real point. That is how the hands are positioned in terms of not being twisted towards one side or other, rather than the means of joining them. Among top players the overlap or Vardon grip as it is also known, is more popular although both Jack Nicklaus and Tiger Woods favour the interlock.

Aiming the Clubface

A well-constructed grip is only as good as the aim of the clubface, so ensure the bottom edge of the face is aimed at right angles to the ball to target line as you begin and end your grip sequence.

A moulded rubber trainer grip is an excellent idea, especially for a beginner.

Fig 32b The interlock grip.

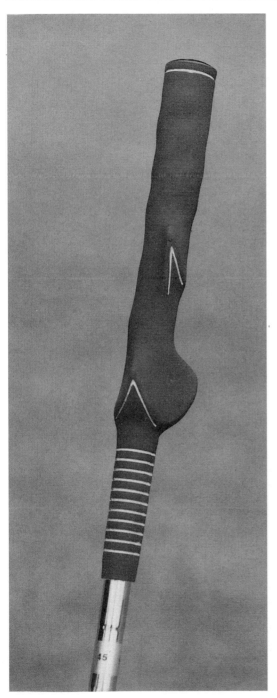

Fig 33 A trainer grip.

Grip Pressure

How hard should you squeeze the club? Holding the club too tight creates tension and limits the natural wrist cock that occurs in the swing. On a scale of one to ten, where ten is tight, normal grip pressure should be around five. World Long Driving Champion Jason Zuback attaches great importance to grip pressure. On the same scale he grips at three.

Finding the ideal grip can take some experimentation. If your shots are curving to the right then the clubface is open (aiming right) at impact. As you take your grip, rotate your hands a little to the right of the centre line on the club as this will help to square the face. If you have been hooking left then your clubface has been closed and you should move the hands left of the centre line.

Aim

Aim of the clubface and body has a strong influence on the swingpath and therefore the start direction of the shot. If you aim to the right, you are likely to swing to the right. However, a player's instinct for the target may make him swing around himself in an attempt to hit the ball on line. While this is reassuring to know, it is far easier to hit straight if you are aiming straight.

Taking Aim

- Good aim begins by setting the clubface at right angles to the ball to target line. This position is known as square. If the face is pointing left, it is closed. Pointing to the right is open.
- Use the grooves on the clubface to help; they aim parallel to the bottom edge.
- Having set the clubface, build your stance around it so the lines of your feet, hips and shoulders run parallel to the ball to target line.

- The shoulders are the most important. To ensure correct shoulder alignment, be clear about two things: 1. Ball position is correct; a ball too far forward opens the shoulders, too far back closes them. 2. The right shoulder has to be lower than the left because the right hand is lower down the handle.

Lay clubs on the floor or use alignment aids to practise. The photo features a magnetic aimer that attaches to the clubface and confirms a square position.

Stance

Stance relates to the width of the feet, weight distribution and the ball position in relation to your body. This position is adjusted to take account of the club being used and whether the shot calls for a descending blow or an upward sweep.

Stance Width and Weight Distribution

- Stance width influences balance and mobility. Too wide and turning is difficult, too narrow and weight shift is compromised.

Fig 34a An excellent start position, assisted by alignment aids.

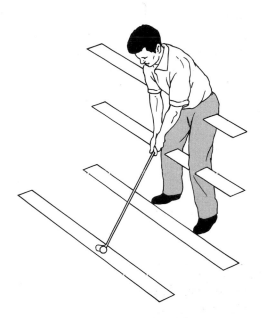

Fig 34b Good body alignment of shoulders, hips and knees.

Angle Your Feet for Added Power

The angle at which your feet are turned out at address can help your swing. To gain resistance in the backswing, keep the back foot at right angles to the target. Turning the back foot outward allows the right knee to move and the hips to turn too much. The front foot however may be flared out by a few degrees as this encourages the hips to clear in the downswing and followthrough.

To feel this for yourself experiment with various foot angles:

Turn your back foot out as far as you can and make a gentle swing, your body will turn too far with no resistance. Through trial and error turn the foot in until you feel coiled in a powerful position. Try the same thing with the front foot and feel how the hip clearance is affected.

WARNING. While experimenting with foot positions, swing with ease as you may be putting your knees and ankles in unfamiliar positions.

For most players the balls of their feet should be between hip and shoulder width apart. Some players successfully widen their stance a little for wood shots while some short shots may require a narrower stance.

- Body weight should be running through the balls of the feet.
- For a full iron shot, spread weight equally between left foot and right, on a wood shot favour the right foot (60 per cent).

Ball Position

- A wood shot from a tee is most easily played with a sweeping or rising hit and should be positioned just inside the left heel.
- An iron from the ground requires a slightly descending blow. This is more easily achieved by playing the ball midway between the feet.

Fig 35a Ball position for a driver.

- The butt end of the club should be opposite the inside of the left thigh for both wood and iron. This helps to achieve the downward hit for an iron as the shaft is leaning a tiny bit forward and promotes an upward hit for a wood.
- For a long iron shot, play from a ball width forward of centre and a fairway wood, two-ball widths forward of centre.

Posture

Posture relates to the way you bend over the ball. Good posture creates a strong and athletic look and it prepares your body to generate power. It also influences the attack angle of your swing, bend over too far and your swing will be steep, stand too vertical and the swing will be flat.

- Bend from the hips, sticking your backside out and bend the knees.
- Many golfers bend from the waist and slouch over the ball. To avoid this, hold a shaft across your hips and push it backwards.
- Good posture allows the arms to hang comfortably in front of your body.
- Once you have established good posture don't take it for granted, check it regularly in a mirror.

Fig 35b (LEFT) *Ball position for a seven iron shot,* (RIGHT) *The butt end of the club is positioned in the same place for driver and seven iron.*

Fig 36 To establish good posture, bend from the hips.

Pre-shot Routine

The GASP skills outlined above are crucial to good golf. However, a skill highly valued by the expert player and overlooked by the novice is the routine. A good routine is a procedure that always follows the same sequence and consistently delivers a correct start position. By observing top players in action you will quickly notice how each one has a routine. Each player's routine is totally individual, and once grooved, will be used on every shot.

It will also be better to keep the routine simple on the basis that it is easier to repeat, so consider the following ideas as you learn to construct your routine.

- Always begin by aiming the clubface, and then forming your grip. But as you lean forward be sure to bend from the hips and not the waist, this will achieve good posture and 'kills two birds with one stone'.

- Build the rest of your stance around the grip and posture.

- Avoid standing like a statue for several seconds, this suggests a long checklist of swing thoughts; you are trying to hit a golf ball not fly an aeroplane!

45

Fig 37 Finding the correct distance from the ball.

Finding the Correct Distance from the Ball

Standing the correct distance from the ball helps to find good posture. Too far away, the knees and body bend too much, too close and everything is too vertical.

Checking distance from the ball couldn't be simpler.

- Take your start position.
- Keep your feet in position and stand upright.
- Settle the clubhead behind the ball and rest the butt end of the club against your left leg.

- If the club is touching your knee, you are standing too far from the ball, if it's touching your pocket you are too close. Good distance from the ball would leave the club resting mid-thigh.

This measure works with every club in the bag; as the club gets longer the shaft pushes you the corresponding distance back from the ball.

- Keep some motion in the routine – this may include shifting weight from foot to foot or using a waggle. This movement helps to begin the swing with smooth take-away and good rhythm. It is extremely difficult to start from a position that has been static for five to ten seconds.

The pre-shot routine will be covered in greater detail in Chapter 5 'On-Course Skills'.

The Pre-shot Routine

An example of a good routine:

1. Aim the clubface with good grip and posture.
2. Position your feet for ball position and alignment.
3. Waggle the club, look at the target and as your eyes return to the ball, begin your swing.

COMMON LONG GAME PROBLEMS

Slicing

The classic definition of a slice is a shot that starts left of target and finishes well right of target, that is, it curves in flight. Many players, with varying degrees of success, accept this shot and use it to their advantage by aiming left in the knowledge that the ball will curve back. The impact or moment of truth that creates the slice features a swingpath that is out to in with a clubface that is open.

The fastest way to cure this problem is to tackle the clubface angle. Often a slicer aims left with his stance, but does he slice because he aims left or does he aim left because he slices? Often the latter. By fixing the clubface so the ball doesn't curve, the player feels no need to aim left.

When the face is open at impact it means that the heel of the club has arrived at the ball before the toe. Due to the geometry of the swing, the heel is leading as the club approaches the ball but the toe has to catch up for a straight shot. In theory, the face of the club automatically squares up at impact as the momentum of the swing uncocks the wrists at the right time. However, since at least 80 per cent of golfers slice, this is an area that needs help.

Practice Drills
Using a six or seven iron:

- On the downswing imagine a race between the heel and the toe, sense the movements that help the toe to win.
- From a position around hip-high on the downswing, try to rotate your right fore-arm over your left through the hitting area. This is a forearm movement and not a hand or wrist movement.

Monitor the flight of the ball. It is only when the ball curves left that the toe has won the race.

As Charlie Sorrell, an American teaching professional says: 'The forearms must cross to show the club who's the boss.'

Hooking

A shot that starts right and finishes left. This shot has a swingpath of out to in with a club-face that is closed. In practical terms the hook can be divided into two, the average player's hook and the expert player's hook.

The average player who hooks nearly always does so because he has a faulty grip. One or both hands are rotated to the right of the centre line on the club which causes the toe to rotate past the heel well before impact and deliver a closed clubface.

In general, the better player hooks because he moves his lower body too fast on the downswing and attacks the ball from in to out. To save the ball from going to the right, his reaction is to close the face pre-impact and create the right to left curve.

Practice Drills

- Check the grip. From the start position look down at the back of the left hand, only two knuckles should be visible and the thumb should be completely covered by the right hand. To achieve this position it may feel like the hands need to rotate left of the centre line of the club.
- In the start position develop the feel of aiming left and then during the swing feel the left arm and left side of the body pulling the club through to the left.
- Check ball position. A hooker often plays the ball too much towards the back foot.

Monitor the ball flight, if the clubface is still closed it will continue curving left.

Shanking

The shank is possibly the most soul-destroying shot in golf, rarely mentioned during the course of play, and then only in a

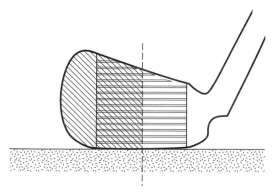

Fig 38 A cure for shanking. Focus on striking the ball with the shaded area.

hushed voice. This is a shot that strikes the ball not with the face, but with the hosel of the club.

Practice Drill

- Using a marker pen draw a vertical line through the centre of your clubface and shade in the toe side of the line. When you swing, try to strike the ball on this half of the club. This small change of focus will produce a centred strike and no more shanking. Shhh. . . .

Topping

The topped shot is exactly that, a shot that has struck the top of the ball. It occurs when the bottom of the swing arrives in the wrong place. It may be too close to the back foot and will therefore be rising when it arrives at the ball just clipping the top. Or it may be bottoming out too far past the ball, so that it just hits directly on top.

Practice Drill

- Take some practice swings and notice where the club wants to hit the ground. If it is too early, then your backswing is probably dominated by your body turn. If this is the case emphasize swinging your arms more upward as you start the swing.
- If the swing bottoms out too late you may be swinging the arms up too much, so emphasize the body turn as you swing back.
- Take some practice swings in slow motion and stop at impact. Notice your body weight. It should be mainly on the front foot, if it is on the back foot then the swing will hit the ground before the ball. In this case you need to start the downswing with a lower body weight shift, just like the side-arm throw.

Summary

As already mentioned there are many individual styles that work very well. There is margin for error – not every golfer has to use exactly the same grip and textbook backswing, but do try to avoid extremes as these require more complicated compensations and, therefore, are difficult to complete with any degree of consistency. Once you have found your own style that gives realistic results, concentrate on the other aspects of golf, short game skills and on-course skills, because this is where the secret of success lies.

CHAPTER 4

Short Game Skills

Short game skills are the second element in the 'Triangle of Success'.

Fig 39 The Triangle of Success.

PUTTING

One of the golfing greats Harry Vardon once referred to putting as, 'The game within a game', thus acknowledging the special skills and techniques required. Other players have put a different twist on this well-known quote by saying: 'Putting is not a game within a game, it *is* the game.'

Hitting the ball long and straight is fun and for many players gives the greatest thrill. However, the driver is used on average fourteen times in a round while putting on its own could contribute up to 50 per cent of the score.

In the early stages of playing golf putting appears unimportant, probably because there seems to be more need to hit the ball in the air and a good distance. There is also less chance of being embarrassed by a poor putt than a poor long shot.

However it is a true sign of development when a pupil asks to have a putting lesson, as this means their long shots are at a stage that offers the chance to score well but that they take too many putts. Amongst tour pros the best putters average around twenty-eight putts per round, that is, ten × two putt and eight × one putt. This is often achieved by excellent shots to the green that leave good one-putt opportunities. For the club player thirty-six putts per round are a good target, that is, ten × two putt, four × one putt and four × three putt.

Recording Your Putts

Use a spare column of the card to record your putts for each hole and find your putts per round. For top level statistics only putts played on the green are counted.

The Key to Good Putting

To achieve consistent putting the real key is learning to judge distance. The line is obviously essential to hole a putt, but if your first putt is always the correct speed then the next putt will be a tap-in. Putting is often seen as individualistic but there are many common denominators that are worth following.

The Grip

The putting grip is rather different from the full swing grip.

Its principal aim is to limit the amount of wrist breakdown, so producing a stroke that rocks from the shoulders in a pendulum style..

The Reverse Overlap

1. Set your hands on the club in a palm-to-palm position, with thumbs on top. Check aim of putter face.
2. Slide your left hand down the club and overlap the index finger over the fingers of the right hand. Check aim again.

Cross-Handed or Left Hand Low (Fig 41)

1. Set your hands on the putter in a palm-to-palm position but with left hand low, and thumbs on top. Check aim.
2. Slide your right hand down the club and overlap the index finger over the fingers of the left hand. Check aim.

Body Position

To achieve the correct pendulum stroke bend forward so that your shoulders are just outside your toes. Let your arms hang comfortably to form your chosen grip. The line across your shoulders should aim parallel to the intended line of putt.

N.B. Many players use putters that are too long. This inhibits good posture and makes the pendulum stroke difficult to achieve. The standard putter length is 35in but many players would benefit from having this shortened by 2 or 3in. If required your golf pro will be able to shorten your putter.

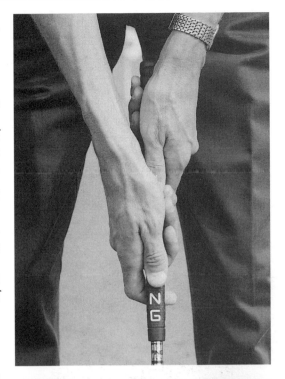

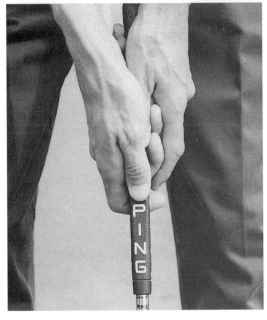

Fig 40 The reverse overlap grip.

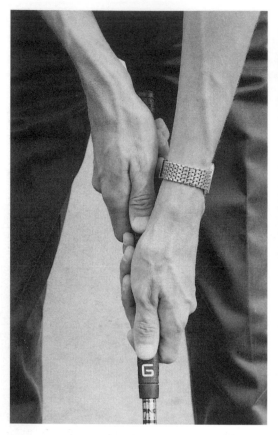 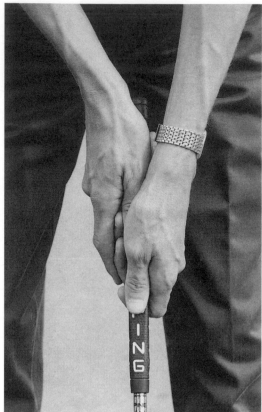

Fig 41 The cross-handed or left-hand low grip.

Ball Position

The ball position should be directly beneath your left eye. To check this, set up to putt and then drop a ball from your eye, if correct it should hit the ball on the ground. This set-up places the ball just forward of centre in the stance, so producing a slight upward stroke.

It also helps aim – if your eyes are outside the target line you will then see the hole left of where it really is and pull the putt left. If your eyes are inside the target line you will push because of misaiming right.

Aim

The putter face needs to be precisely aimed along the intended line of putt. On a curving putt you must choose your line and stay with it. It is very easy to set up along the intended line, but as you settle allow the face to drift towards the hole and therefore 'under-borrow' and finish on the low side. Try to identify a mark on the putting surface on your line about 2ft ahead of the ball. Then roll the ball over it.

Note: When selecting a putter, choose a style that features a sighting line to make aim as easy as possible.

Fig 42 Drop a ball from your left eye to check the ball position.

Putting Drill for Aim

Practise with a putting string (*see* Fig 43). Set the ball under the string with the logo pointing at the hole. Take your stance, if your eyes are in the correct position, the string will appear directly above the logo. Look along the line to see perfect aim and then putt.

The Stroke

While many different strokes are witnessed, it is widely agreed that the most consistent style is the pendulum stroke. This is a simple combination of arms and shoulders swinging as a unit without any independent wrist movement. This action produces excellent distance control as there is no conscious hit, just a smooth acceleration.

Imagine a triangle across your shoulders and down both arms, now simply move this shape in a rocking motion keeping your head still, follow through the same length as your backswing and you will have a great putting stroke. An excellent grip and body position will help achieve the pendulum stroke.

Reading Greens

Look for the overall contours as you approach the green. When the ball is rolling quickly, a slope doesn't affect it as much as when it slows down. So when reading a putt the final 6ft, as it slows, is where you can anticipate most of the break.

Watch carefully when your playing partners putt, especially as the ball slows down. But be sure not to stand on an extension of their line as this is against the rules of golf.

Fig 43 Using a putting string to achieve perfect aim.

Putter Designs

There are thousands of putter designs available but the two main features to understand are:

1. Hard or soft feel
2. Weight/balance

The material of the face determines the feel of the putter. It may be a hard steel, or it may have a special insert that gives a soft feel, designed to give improved feedback (because the ball is in contact with the putter for longer) and therefore better distance control.

WARNING: Soft insert putters are not recommended on slow greens.

To test the weighting of any putter, balance the shaft carefully on one finger and look at the clubhead. If the face is looking to the sky it is a face-balanced design. If the toe is hanging down towards the ground it is a toe-weighted style. Possibly the most common is something in between. Face-balanced suits a stroke that swings in a straight line, toe-weighted suits a stroke that swings from inside the line of the putt so that the extra toe weight helps to return the face on line.

Distance Control

Striking the putter in its sweet spot is crucial to good judgement of distance. Heel or toe strikes will leave the ball short and possibly off line. To encourage good striking pick out a single dimple on the ball and keep your eye fixed until well after impact.

Fig 44 A sound putting stroke, using the shoulders rather than the wrists.

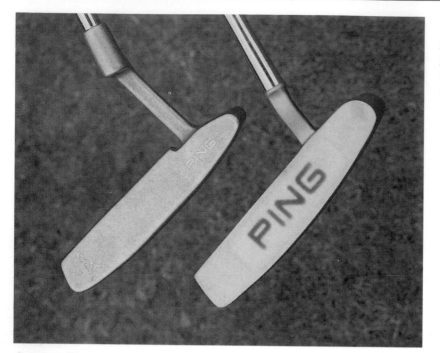

Fig 45 Two very popular styles of putter featuring different clubface materials.

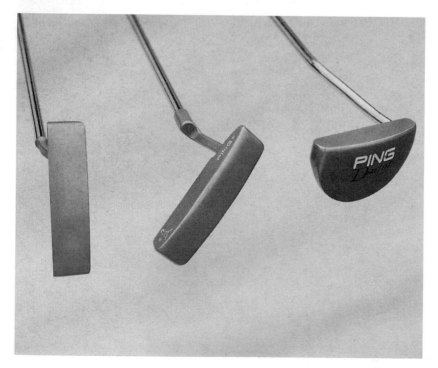

Fig 46 A toe-weighted putter on the left and a face-balanced putter on the right.

Putting Drill for Distance

Lay a club on the green approximately 10ft away and then a second 20ft away.

Round 1. Hit a putt that goes just past the first club, then another that goes midway between the clubs, then a third ball that finishes just short of the second club.

Round 2. Introduce a fourth ball and as before advance the distance with each putt, without going past the end club.

Round 3. Add a fifth ball etc. . . .

As you need to hit the putt further add more backswing but keep a similar tempo, rather than using the same length swing and hitting with a different tempo.

Putting Drill for Holing Out

Place a tee 3ft from the hole and hole out three consecutive putts. Continue until you have completed ten repetitions, that is, thirty putts holed. If you miss on twenty-nine you must start again at one. Stay on the green until you have finished.

Ben Crenshaw on Putting

Ben Crenshaw, one of the finest putters in golf sums up putting in a simple way:

'Don't try too hard to hole every putt. A must make attitude puts too much pressure on your stroke . . . Just do your best to get the correct line and speed and roll the ball at the hole on that line.'

CHIPPING AND PITCHING

The best players in the world miss on average about six greens in regulation per round yet still score par or better. This is largely due to excellent short shots followed by solid putting.

Fig 47 A putting drill for distance control.

Fig 48 A putting drill for holing out.

The eighteen handicap club player may miss all eighteen greens in regulation and face fourteen or fifteen short approach shots. If he could get down in two on 30 per cent of these holes he could reduce his score by five strokes per round without having to improve his long game.

Shot selection is key for all scoring zone situations. In general, a ball rolling close to the ground is easier to control than one in the air and a lower, shorter swing is easier to control than a higher, more vertical one.

> ### Selecting the Safest Option
>
> Putt if you can.
> If you can't putt then chip.
> If you can't chip then pitch.

CHIPPING

A key concept in chipping is to see the shot as part of the putting family. It is a simple extension of a long putt using a seven or eight iron to give some loft that will carry the ball over the fringe so it may begin to roll towards the flag.

The Set-Up

The set-up position for chipping involves using the putting position with some minor adjustments. The ball should be played further back, just inside the back foot, body weight should be slightly left-sided and the handle ahead of the ball. Each of these tweaks encourages a downward strike on the ball and reduces the chance of fluffing.

In addition, many leading players use their specialist putting grip when chipping. This will feel awkward initially but try it in practice and you will see how it helps to reduce unwanted wrist action.

Fig 49 The chipping stance.

N.B. Grip low down the handle which will allow you to stand close to the ball and use a light grip pressure to enhance feel.

The Stroke

Like putting the chipping action works well with a simple pendulum stroke. This involves rocking the shoulders and allowing the arms to swing gently with no conscious wrist action. Moving the triangle back and forth is an excellent image and will help your impact position match your start position.

Lanny Wadkins, former US Ryder Cup Captain says: 'Basically I chip the way I putt . . . The most important factor in making the chipping stroke is keeping both wrists fixed'.

Fig 50 Simple chip shots mimic a putting stroke.

The Chip-Stick

The chip-stick is a training aid that highlights excess wrist movement. Simply inserted into the shaft through the hole in the end of the grip, the chip-stick will nudge the player in the ribs when the wrists flick the club at the ball.

In the photo the stroke is played well and there is no contact with the body.

Distance Control

Judging the correct amount of strength for a chip is similar to judging a putt, however there is an additional variable – loft on the club.

A putter has only 2–4 degrees of loft while your chipping club has 36 degrees if using a seven iron or 40 degrees for an eight iron.

To gain consistent distance control the loft at impact also needs to be consistent. This is achieved in two ways:

Fig 51 The chip-stick.

1. Using the simple pendulum stroke. If the wrists are active loft can be increased by scooping, or reduced by squeezing at impact.
2. Using the same club. This is a choice between seven or eight iron. Practise with both, choose one and stick to it.

Having made your choice, recognize the carry to roll ratio of the shot. In normal ground conditions you should find that the ball will carry around one-third the distance and roll the remainder. Once you are familiar with this ratio then shot execution becomes a lot easier. Judge where the first bounce is required and this will give a much better visual image than just looking from the ball to the hole.

Practice Drill
When practising lay a towel on the green at the point you want to land the ball. This helps to fine-tune your carry to roll ratio and build a strong mental picture of the shot.

Controlling the Speed on Chip Shots

Be prepared for changes in course conditions. The speed and texture of the greens will affect the strength of your chip shots so before you tee off try some chips onto the practice green.

The Chip-Pitch (Fig 56b)

This would be the shot to use when playing to a tight pin position with little green to use.

The chip-pitch is a short lofted shot (25yd or less), played with chipping technique and a very lofted club.

To develop distance control, repeat the steps taken in chipping practice and trust the loft of the club!

PITCHING

Pitching covers shots that are longer and higher than chips but not as far as shots played with a full swing. This 'in between' shot can cause confusion and frustration as a poorly played shot turns attack into defence in one bad swing.

For this length of shot the basic pendulum swing will not supply enough power so a wrist hinge has to be added to allow the club to travel further and achieve greater force.

The Set-Up

A pitch requires the normal grip used on all full-swing shots although the position up or down the handle will vary to suit the length of shot. The stance needs to be slightly narrower

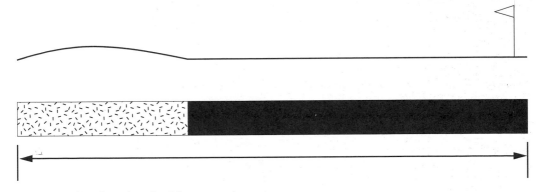

Fig 52a A chip shot played with a seven iron.

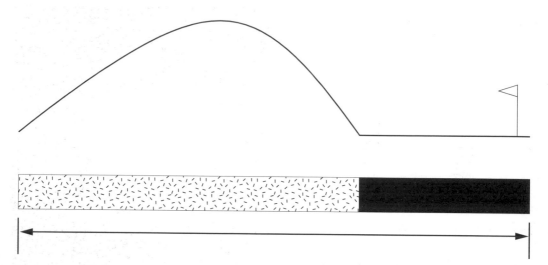

Fig 52b A chip-pitch played with a pitching wedge.

than for a full swing with the ball positioned between the heels. Body weight should be 60 per cent on the left foot. The line of the feet should aim slightly left to promote the wrist action and help the body turn through.

The Swing

To develop a good repeating strike on the ball the club has to be delivered back to the same place each time. The most consistent method for achieving this is using 'The Dead Hands Swing'. This style uses basic forces working in the swing (momentum and gravity) to return the club to the correct position.

Using a light grip pressure make a half-length backswing with a full wrist hinge and then on the downswing turn through allowing your arms and wrists to drop down to the ball and on to a full finish. Initially this may feel unnerving as you may have been tightening up in the past, but trust the club to unhinge with the swing and you will experience superb, softly flighted pitches.

Fig 53 The pitching stance.

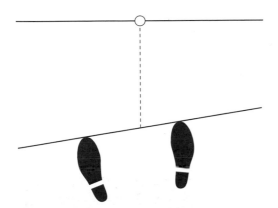

Fig 54 Aim feet left of target line.

Develop a relaxed rhythm that allows the body and not the arms to control the speed. The hands help to deliver the power but don't add power.

Errors to Avoid

Inexperienced players try to help the ball up by scooping with the hands. More established players know not to scoop but often go too much the other way and de-loft the club at impact.

Feel the Bounce

When you deliver the club perfectly you will feel the sole of the club gliding through. This is called the bounce that provides greater margin for error. If the angle of attack is too steep, the front edge of the sole will dig in to the turf and cause inconsistent contact and poor distance control.

The Wrist Cock

To help feel a wrist cock, take your stance and by using your wrists only, try to touch the club against your head. This vertical action is a wrist cock.

Fig 55a Scooping, hands too far back at impact.

Distance Control

Many players judge distance by feel, that is, they estimate how far away the flag is then make a swing that they feel will hit the required length based on past experience.

Fig 55b De-lofting, hands too far forward at impact.

Fig 55c A good impact position.

Fig 56 A nine
o'clock backswing.

An alternative method is to learn a pre-set length of backswing and know how far it will hit the ball.

A convenient measure is to imagine standing with your back towards a giant clock face, now swing back until your left arm is at nine o'clock.

Then swing the club through with the dead hands style.

Follow this three-step sequence to develop your skill:

Step 1

Using a pitching wedge, learn to make a nine o'clock swing. Practise with a partner for feedback and encouragement.

Continue to practise until you can consistently achieve good contact and trajectory.

This may take as little as forty shots but could need considerably more.

Step 2

Record how far well-struck shots carry.

This can be achieved by pacing out and laying down clubs at set distances i.e. 50, 60 and 70yd and then noting down where a well-struck shot lands. Only record well-struck shots that achieve the correct trajectory.

After hitting around twenty-five shots you

Change of Position on the Handle for Added Control

When using a nine o'clock swing, position your grip in the middle of the handle. When using a shorter backswing, grip down lower for extra control and when using a longer swing use the full length of the club to help provide more power.

---

will begin to see a regular distance. Keep a note of this, then return on another day to double check. (If your distances are erratic return to Step 1.)

The exact distance for a pitching wedge/nine o'clock swing will vary from player to player. However, the majority of men will carry 50–70yd and ladies a little shorter.

If your distance is 60yd then you can practise, develop consistency and have a great anchor point for your game.

Fig 57 Hitting a longer pitch shot.

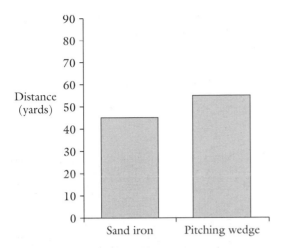

Fig 58 Typical pitching distances using a nine o'clock backswing.

Step 3

Learn to *change the time* on your backswing to hit longer or shorter shots. From an anchor point of 60yd you would know that a shot requiring a carry of 70yd needs a backswing of more than nine o'clock.

Having gained confidence with a pitching wedge try to repeat the above steps using your sand iron. (It will be a lot easier second time around).

Once you have established some consistency, to help remember your yardages stick a label on the shaft of each club with your nine o'clock distance.

Learning the simple nine o'clock anchor point for two clubs will give you tremendous confidence and consistency for these 'in between' shots.

BUNKER SHOTS

There are many club players who turn to jelly at the prospect of playing from a bunker. However, understanding the basic principles coupled with a small amount of practice can make a large improvement.

Walter Hagen, winner of eleven major championships said: 'The bunker shot is the easiest shot in golf – you don't even have to hit the ball.'

The Concept

Hit the sand, not the ball. Why?

Trying to play the ball without touching the sand is fraught with danger. If you decide to play the shot as a chip, just a few grains of sand between club and ball will cushion the impact and only move the ball a few feet. As the ball will often 'settle down' in the sand, attempting to hit the ball first gives a small target with high risk. Therefore, make the decision to use the splash shot, that is, to play the sand with the ball using a more powerful swing than a chip shot. This offers considerably more margin for error as the contact point into the sand can vary by several inches yet still produce a safe shot.

Equipment

Execution of the splash shot is made possible by the design of the sand iron. Back in 1932 American golfer Gene Sarazen was concerned about his bunker play. One day while thinking about this he noticed how the design of an aeroplane wing has the trailing edge lower than the leading edge, with the air resistance against this surface creating lift. Would this same effect work in sand?

He had solder put on the sole of several wedges ensuring that the back edge was lower than the front. After much fine-tuning he was happy and during that year he won both the British and US Opens with the help of some excellent bunker play.

The modern 'bounce sole' sand iron had been born.

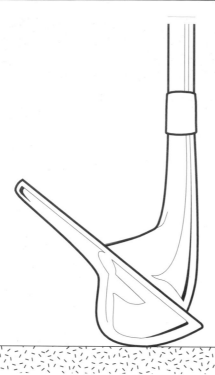

Fig 59 A sand iron; notice that the back edge of the sole is much lower than the front edge.

The Set-Up

Aim feet and shoulders slightly left of target and establish firm footing by shuffling feet into sand.

Position ball towards front foot, because contact needs to be with the sand before the ball.

Aim face of club towards flag and then grip. By taking the grip at this point the face will be open which adds even more bounce to the club. The grip will feel rotated to the left of its normal position on the handle.

Point the handle of the club towards your tummy button.

Body weight should favour the left foot.

The Swing

Once set up, the direction of swing should be along the line of your body, slightly left of target. Aim to make contact 2–4in before the ball safe in the knowledge that the sole will glide through the sand allowing the ball to pop out with a high soft flight. The swing needs to be free flowing with a positive acceleration through to the finish.

Don't Touch the Sand

The Rules of Golf do not allow you to touch the sand as you prepare or set up to play, so be sure to hover the clubhead so as not to incur a penalty.

Fig 60a Playing a splash shot from a greenside bunker.

Fig 60b Playing a splash shot from a greenside bunker.

Distance Control

Distance control for bunker shots can be achieved in a number of different ways. Length of backswing, amount of sand that is taken and speed of swing are factors. Also, changing the face angle, that is, more open for short shots, is another option.

However, learning to hit a 15yd bunker shot consistently will put you safely on the green and close to the flag in the majority of situations.

Practice Drill
Using your finger, draw a circle in the sand and simply practise splashing this island out of

Fig 61 (LEFT AND BELOW) Splash the island of sand out of the bunker and the ball will go with it.

the bunker. Repeat this ten times and then put a ball in the middle of the circle, try exactly the same swing and the ball will come out.

This develops feel for the resistance of sand, the bounce of your club and confirms that you often can't even sense contact with the ball.

The Plugged Lie

Occasionally a ball may stay in its own pitch mark. This requires a different shot known as the Explosion Shot. In this situation using the bounce sole would prevent the club from digging down deep enough to reach the bottom of the ball, so now the face should be held square or slightly closed with the ball in the centre of the stance. This creates a steeper angle of attack and therefore more resistance

from the sand thus requiring a very aggressive hit. The ball will come out with overspin and therefore runs on much further than a splash shot.

The change of ball position from the splash to the explosion shot is shown in Fig 62.

One of the greatest exponents of the bunker shot is Gary Player. After holing out from a greenside bunker he once overheard somebody comment that it was lucky. Gary replied, 'the more I practise the luckier I get!' How often do you practise bunker shots?

Fairway Bunker Shots

When faced with a shot from a fairway bunker the objective is no longer to hit the sand first. A fairway bunker shot requires greater

Fig 62 Change the ball position to suit the lie.

distance than the greenside shot and therefore clean contact with the ball is required. Before executing the shot there are some important considerations:

- The lie of the ball – if the ball is lying in, rather than on the sand, you must accept that it will not be possible to gain significant distance, so use a sand iron for a simple splash shot. If the ball is sitting on top then consider the height of the lip and the yardage before selecting the club.
- The height of the bunker lip – sometimes a fairway bunker may feature a lip so shallow that a fairway wood can be used, but more often the lip will limit club selection. Determine the straightest club that would successfully clear the lip and then look at the yardage.
- The yardage to the green – a situation may be such that you require a five iron to achieve the correct length but need the loft of an eight iron for sufficient elevation to clear the bunker lip, in which case you must accept that the green is out of range. When deciding on the club, also consider that the technique will deliver slightly less power

than a normal full swing played from the fairway.

If in doubt about which club to select, always opt for the more lofted choice. It is far better to be safe than sorry.

The Set-Up
Grip lower down the handle than normal and establish a good solid foothold. The right foot is especially important, as it needs to provide stability for the downswing. Position the ball in the centre of the stance with your body weight favouring the left foot.

The Swing
The ideal swing involves sweeping the ball cleanly away. A thinned contact is better than too much sand. A passive leg action and a three-quarter length swing will help a player to keep their height and pick the ball off the surface. Attempting to hit hard is particularly risky, as balance can easily be lost; it requires only a few grains of sand between clubface and ball to seriously affect the outcome of the shot.

CHAPTER 5
On-Course Skills

If there is any particular secret to good golf it may be found within the content of this chapter. The skills covered include: thinking like a champion, course management, assessing your own game, improving through quality practice and dealing with interesting situations and conditions. Each of these important elements will help to equip you with improved on-course skills and assist in developing your golf.

On-course skills are the third and final element in the 'Triangle of Success'.

Fig 63 The Triangle of Success.

THINKING LIKE A CHAMPION

Golf is a difficult game and during any round, you will hit shots that you are not pleased with. The solution to this problem however is to realize that, whoever you are, you cannot totally avoid these shots, but that the challenge is the manner in which you respond.

The way in which a golfer sees himself and any situation is his choice. Some players choose to look on the dark side, frequently feeling that luck is against them and dwelling on bad shots. While others accept what has happened, they may not like it, but they enjoy the challenge of doing something about it. Which attitude is likely to help you play better golf and allow you to enjoy it? There are a number of simple mental skills that good players use and these are available to you too.

The Pre-shot Routine

The sound pre-shot routine as already mentioned in Chapter 3, is something that will benefit every golfer. In this section it is broken down to help you understand what, when and why things happen so that you can sharpen up your own routine. It will help decision-making, develop consistency and occupy the mind in a constructive fashion. While each player will have his own individual routine, it will always include two elements, preparation and execution.

The Preparation Phase
The preparation phase of a golf shot begins as the player arrives at his ball, it is during this phase that he needs to analyse the situation

and decide upon the best way to play the shot. He has to select which club to use; this will be based on the yardage, the lie of the ball, wind direction, any changes in elevation and his own personal feel for the shot. He also has to decide on where to aim and then on the best technique to use.

Selecting a Target

Legendary teaching professional Harvey Penick said, 'Take dead aim.' Always select a target, for instance on a tee shot be specific, just aiming at the fairway encourages a scatter gun approach, think instead like a marksman. Pick out a small target – the tree trunk, not just the tree itself; this instinctively encourages you to be more accurate.

Visualization

This is the skill that involves seeing the shot in your mind, thus creating an image that the body can respond to. In particular, see the target, get connected to the target and allow your senses to help your swing. The high handicap player often gets locked into the ball and barely glances at the target. For him the ball is the target, but ignoring the real target in this way not only creates problems with alignment, but it gives his senses little opportunity to gather information so the body really doesn't know what to do. It's like trying to play in the dark.

'I never hit a shot, not even in practice, without having a very sharp picture of it in my head', said Jack Nicklaus, winner of eighteen major championships.

The Execution Phase

Having made these decisions the player is ready to execute. This phase includes picturing or visualizing the shot and will usually include a practice swing to help you to relax and to feel the shot, followed by the set-up and swing sequence that the individual player uses. As each player begins their swing, they should have a simple image or thought that they know and trust to help them hit a good shot.

A Common Problem

During post-round interviews you will sometimes hear a leading player talk about hitting a bad shot because of a mental error; this will often be a case of that player not making a positive decision during preparation and so not committing to the execution. Among club players this is one of the most common causes of a bad shot. The following scenario would be typical:

Harry is chatting to Mike as he arrives at his ball on the fairway, he notices that he is level with the 150yd marker and decides on a six iron. He continues chatting as he takes his stance and then looking up from the ball, he notices the flag is towards the back of the green. He thinks that maybe he needs a five iron but decides to hit a hard six. Then he feels a gust of wind; conscious that he has already dwelt over the ball for a long time he decides that he'll hit the six iron anyway. He tries to swing much harder than normal and seriously mishits the ball into trouble. Harry should have made his decisions about the shot as he prepared so that the execution would feel straightforward. When players visit the practice range they often hit better shots than on the course because they are simply executing; they haven't needed to decide, so committing to the shot is far easier.

Building Your Routine

Set a personal goal of using a two-step routine for every shot you play.

First, prepare by assessing the shot and making the necessary decisions. Second, trust

Fig 64a Preparing to tee off.

the decision and commit to the shot. This will begin to define in your mind the discipline of decision-making.

Lack of Commitment

A wrong decision is better than not committing. Failure to commit will cause more bad results than making a poor decision. If you have chosen the wrong club the ball may finish 10–12yd away, however not committing yourself will be far worse and will produce a bad strike.

Fig 64b Preparing to tee off.

The next time you play, maintain the same two-step approach, but notice your mannerisms when in the execution mode. For instance, does a practice swing relax you, where do you take a practice swing, do you waggle the club, how many times do you look at the target? As you recognize the things that you tend to do, try to repeat them on each shot. You are building a pre-shot routine. At the end of your game think through the sequence in your mind so that you can easily remember for the next time. Please note – a routine that is short and simple is far better than one which is long and complicated, it is easier to repeat and gives the player less opportunity to second guess themselves.

It's Not Just Physical
Using the same physical habits is also programming the mind to follow a pattern so that it is less likely to be distracted by any

situation. A tournament player leans heavily on his routine, he knows that by repeating the same sequence on every shot, it affords him a protection against pressure. In the closing stages of a tournament this is very welcome and often crucial to his overall success.

A Sample Routine

1. Preparation; analyse the situation, make a positive decision on the type of shot, club selection and choose a small target.
2. Execute; visualize a superb shot, take a practice swing to help feel the shot that you have just seen, adopt your set-up position, waggle the club, have one more look at the target and swing.

Be positive, see a great shot and just do it!

Stay in the Present

Strongly linked to the pre-shot routine, is staying in the present, or playing one shot at a time which is another crucial aspect of on-course skill. When a player is scoring well he is tempted to plan far ahead, he may say to himself 'All I need to do is par the last hole and I'm bound to win.' He may even be thinking about the people whom he needs to thank in his acceptance speech!

Alternatively, in a poor round he may dwell on a bad shot that he has just played and take that image with him into the next shot, with the inevitable outcome.

Champion golfers have a wonderful habit of putting bad shots behind them. They achieve this by concentrating on what they are doing. Getting on with what needs to be done to hit the next shot will put thoughts of the score, or how the round is going, out of their mind. A simple task like scraping dirt from their spikes can occupy the mind and help the player to stay in the present.

A consistent pre-shot routine helps enormously as this returns the player to the job in hand.

Concentration

Club players often play from the first tee and stride off down the fairway with a furrowed brow, deep in concentration. This is a tough way to play, as retaining this level of concentration for eighteen holes is a real challenge. The simple requirement of concentration in golf is that you are thinking about the right thing at the right time. So relax between shots, chat to your partners and as Walter Hagen famously remarked, 'Don't forget to smell the roses.'

The Little Voice in Your Head

The duration of a round of golf is normally between three and four hours, thus regardless of the player's standard, there is lots of thinking time between shots. The way a player thinks about himself can influence his performance. Whether you think you are going to play well, or whether you think you are going to play badly, either way you will be right.

Cultivating a good self-image is key. A player who thinks of himself as a good putter probably is, while the player who thinks that he is a bad putter undoubtedly will be. The little voice in your head contributes to your self-image and these messages are often negative.

For example: Harry and Mike are playing together as partners in a four-ball competition. They are playing well and on the last hole have a chance to win. Harry tees off first and hits out of bounds, Mike hits a good drive straight down the middle. Mike, playing an eight iron to the green, tops the ball and it rolls about 30yd. How should Harry react?

If he called Mike an idiot, told him he had a hopeless swing and knew that he couldn't

Swindon Libraries
North Swindon Library
Orbital Shopping Park
01793 707120
Visit www.swindon.gov.uk/libraries

Borrowed Items 24/07/2015 10:55
XXXXX04006

Item Details   Due Date
Golf   14/08/2015
women's golf handbook :   14/08/2015
the complete guide to
improving your game

Thank you for using
North Swindon Library

play under pressure it certainly would not help. But those are the things that Mike would be saying to himself. Instead, Harry would most likely reassure his partner that he is playing well and that the next shot to the green is one of his favourites. Harry would know that he needs to be supportive towards his partner for him to make a good recovery.

The next time the little voice in your head threatens to say something harmful, remember that you would not make the same remark to your partner and therefore consciously respond with a positive comment.

The Book of Good Shots
An excellent way to build your self-image as a golfer, is to keep a book of good shots. After each game think through the round hole by hole, as many players do, and list the shots that you were pleased with. Record the hole number and the club you used, cover the whole range of shots including putts. Some players debrief by remembering vividly the bad shots in the belief that this will help eliminate them, but this approach leaves images of failure that do not foster improvement.

This book of good shots will become a source of encouragement and by visiting it the evening before you play will provide a wonderful boost in confidence.

Visit Your Personal Library

An alternative would be to have a mental library that contains the best shot that you have ever played with each of your clubs (a maximum of fourteen). When preparing for a shot, visit the library and visualize the image of the great shot that *you* played with that same club. When you hit one that is even better, simply swap the new for the old.

The manner in which a player responds to a shot or situation is always their choice. A person with a positive attitude, after an excellent round, might have some of the following thoughts; 'That's like me', 'I can do that again', 'I am a good player.' However, someone with the opposite attitude may respond to the same performance by saying to himself; 'That must have been a fluke' or 'I don't suppose I'll be able to do that again.' These differing approaches reinforce the way in which each player sees himself, thus helping the positive player to improve while holding back the negative player, even after a good performance.

After a poor performance the response may be even more important. The positive player may think 'That's not like me', 'I'm going to play better than that next time' and 'Even the very best players have off days.' While the contrasting approach might include 'I always play that way', 'That's just typical' or 'I really am hopeless.'

Remember the response is up to you, decide which attitude will help you to improve, enjoy your game more, and consciously practise doing it.

Changing the Way You Think

If you recognize some of these tendencies in yourself, the good news is that *you can* change the way you think. Tony Buzan, an expert on the workings of the mind, suggests considering your mind as an enormous neural jungle full of different routes and options. The route that you presently use is well-trodden and offers the obvious path. However, to change the way you think, picture yourself as an adventurer searching out a new and better route. At first this route is hard and takes extra effort, but each time this path is used it becomes flattened. Very soon the old route gets overgrown and the new route is the obvious and easier one to follow. In this way you can change your thoughts. It requires some conscious initial effort, for instance, during your mental debrief after a round only remember good shots. This will feel difficult if you have traditionally pondered the bad ones, but focus on these good shots, if necessary revisiting the same good shots over and over. Follow the same ritual after each time you play and after four or five games your new thought process will be on its way to being automatic.

Summary of Thinking Like a Champion

Good mental skills aid good golf, adopt a positive attitude towards your game and decide that you are going to play well. Don't just wait and see, make it happen.
Ability is what you can do.
Motivation is what you do do.
Attitude is how well you do it.

COURSE MANAGEMENT

The mental skills that have been outlined in 'Thinking Like a Champion' play a very significant role in course management. There are also specific skills associated with managing your game on the course. These revolve around just a couple of straightforward ideas:

1. Play to your strengths – that is, when deciding on the type of shot to play, always favour a choice that, based on past performance, has a high percentage success rate.
2. Choose a target that allows you maximum margin for error. This policy doesn't require the player to hit the perfect shot every time.

Leading sports psychologist, Dr Bob Rotella, uses the expression 'conservative strategy, cocky swing'. This means that by deciding to play a conservative shot, one that you have executed with success on many previous occasions will give a feeling of confidence and is very likely to produce another good shot. The reverse of this approach would be a cocky strategy, conservative swing. This is much less likely to produce a good shot because opting for a high-risk choice a player may well feel apprehensive and not commit himself as he should.

Playing on the Course

To cover how these simple ideas operate on the course, let's follow two players around a few holes. Firstly an introduction to our players:

Jim is fifty-five years of age, has an eleven handicap. He has played golf for many years and would love to reduce his handicap to single figures. He is planning early retirement when he hopes to be able to achieve his goal.

Simon is twenty-two, and has only been playing golf for a year. He is very strong and hits the ball a long way, although not consistently. His goal is to score under a hundred.

Hole 1.
Par 4. 330yd.

This is a classic opening hole, fairly short in length and inviting the player out onto the course.

Jim selects a three wood, rather than his driver, because he knows it offers greater margin for error and the hole doesn't require a particularly long drive. He hits a good shot 210yd down the middle.

Simon chooses a driver because he enjoys hitting the ball a long way. He swings hard and makes good contact but the ball slices to the right and finishes in the rough.

When the players arrive at their balls Simon is surprised to see that he has been outdriven by Jim's three wood. Simon now faces a shot of 130yd to the centre of the green, with a

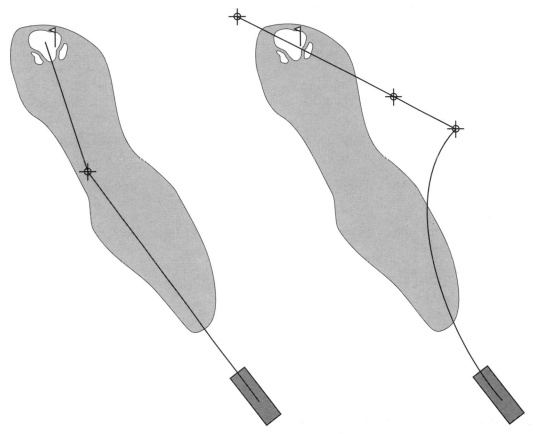

Fig 65 (LEFT) Jim playing hole 1. (RIGHT) Simon playing hole 1.

greenside bunker on his line to the flag. He chooses an eight iron and aims directly at the flag. Taking no account of the lie, he catches too much grass between club and ball only advancing 50yd.

Jim has 120yd to go, also selecting an eight iron he plays nicely on to the green.

Simon, still in the rough, now has 80yd remaining and decides to hit a hard sand iron. Determined to make sure that he doesn't catch too much grass this time, he strikes the ball half way up, with the result that it never gets more than 10ft into the air and overshoots the green into some bushes.

He finds his ball and after a penalty drop manages to finish the hole in seven. Jim makes a comfortable two putt for his par four.

Walking to the second, Jim feels comfortable while Simon feels as if he has already blown his chances of breaking the hundred barrier.

What went wrong?
Simon made strategic errors on each of his three shots.

● He chose to hit a driver from the tee. For a player of Simon's standard and experience he doesn't need to use a driver on any hole, a three wood will be more consistent and still hit the ball far enough. For golfers of nearly all standards the tee shot is about putting the ball in play.

- On his second shot the ball was lying in the rough and he didn't consider any adjustment to take this into account. He also chose to aim directly at the flag placed behind a bunker. Even with a good shot the ball was likely to roll over the back of the green as playing from the rough limits the amount of backspin that can be imparted. So taking the risk of going over the bunker had no potential gain. Simon should have assessed the lie as part of his preparation, possibly deciding to position the ball further back in his stance so reducing the amount of contact with the grass at impact. Then he should have chosen to aim at the opening to the green thus avoiding the bunkers. When selecting his club he could have used a nine iron instead of an eight. The adjusted ball position tends to de-loft the club and encourage the ball to run a little further. With this plan in mind Simon would then have been able to visualize the shot landing short of the green and rolling up and onto the front edge or just short – either way leaving a simple third shot. This would be a classic example of a conservative strategy encouraging a cocky swing.
- When Simon came to play his original third shot he made another mistake. He was thinking about the previous shot too much, rather than staying in the present. He should recognize what went wrong with the previous shot and then take a practice swing to feel the resistance from the grass and tune in to the shot at hand.

Despite choosing poorly from the tee Simon had the chance to play a good second shot but made the wrong choice and then on his third shot compounded the error further. This gives a good example of why Simon is yet to score below a hundred.

Hole 2.
Par 4. 450yd.

A very tough hole. A straightforward tee shot but 50yd short of the green a series of cross bunkers wait menacingly.

Jim has the honour and with his driver hits a superb shot 230yd down the middle.

Simon seeing this and thinking that for such a long hole he needs a very long drive also chooses his driver. Sadly he attempts to hit too hard and tops the ball just past the ladies' tee about 40yd ahead. When Simon arrives at his ball he recognizes that the lie is not good and selects a nine iron. He gets a decent contact and is surprised to see how far the ball travels. It is still Simon's turn to play and he hits an excellent five wood.

Jim has hit a very good drive leaving 220yd to go, although in the fairway, his ball is sitting on a rather bare lie and he is concerned about being able to carry the cross bunkers. He is so tempted by the prospect of telling his friends that he reached the green in two that he decides to take the shot on and selects his three wood. In his eagerness to get the shot over with he fails to complete his backswing correctly and strikes the ball in the heel of the club so that it flies low with a fade and rolls into one of the cross bunkers.

Simon finds his ball with 140yd remaining and opts for a seven iron, his favourite club. Buoyed up by the misfortune of Jim, he hits a solid shot onto the green.

Poor Jim, who just a few moments earlier was looking forward to boasting about being on the green in two, would now be delighted to reach the green in three. The 50yd bunker shot is recognized as the hardest shot in golf, a fact of which Jim is well aware. In playing

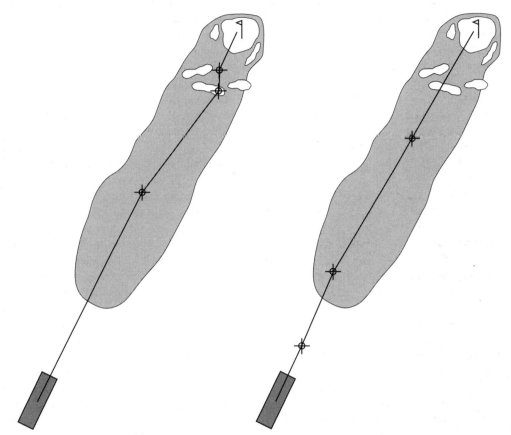

Fig 66 (LEFT) Jim playing hole 2. (RIGHT) Simon playing hole 2.

the shot he takes too much sand, the ball escapes the bunker but remains 30yd short of the green. Jim gathers himself together, pitches on and two putts for a six. Simon takes two putts, also for a six.

What went wrong?

- A player should have a realistic gameplan for each hole. For Jim using his handicap, his plan for this hole should be: on the green in three, two putts and move on to the next. The number on the scorecard is the only thing that counts. This may have been his intention, but after hitting a very good drive he got carried away and took on a shot that carried a high risk. Sadly he paid the price by dropping two shots, so after playing two holes and only hitting one bad shot, he is two over par. Jim should have decided to hit short of the cross bunkers and leave a simple approach.
- Simon's goal of breaking a hundred means that he doesn't need to try to reach long

par four holes in two shots. In fact, an excellent gameplan for any beginner is to try and reach the green in the par of the hole and then two putt. If this was achieved on every hole the player would score just over a hundred, but the reality is that they would be able to reach most holes in less than par and so lower their score without taking on unrealistic shots. Simon mishit his tee shot because he tried to hit it too hard. However he played to his strengths on the other shots and completed the hole very well.

Hole 3.
Par 3. 200yd.

A challenging hole with lots of trouble around the green. There is a gentle breeze blowing against and slightly from the left.

Jim to begin with, is not sure about which club to use, either three or five wood. He reasons that due to the breeze he needs the three. He makes a positive decision and commits to the shot, knowing that anything less is destined for trouble. He ignores the flag that is located on the left edge of the green and instead takes aim at a small bush directly behind the centre of the green. He visualizes the shot, takes a practice swing to feel it and then executes a perfect three wood onto the centre of the green. Simon knows that he can also hit the ball that far and opts for his three wood but it slices into a greenside bunker.

Simon is greeted by his ball sitting very close to the back lip of the bunker and is forced to play away from the green. From there he plays a weak chip shot leaving a long putt. He takes three more to get down, six in all!

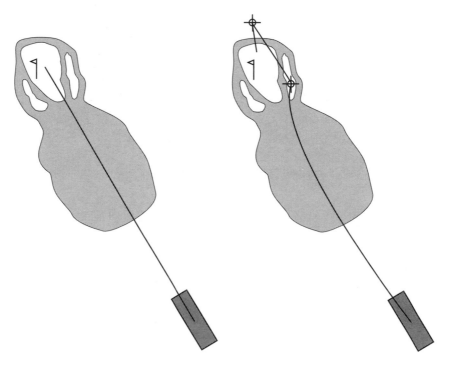

Fig 67 (LEFT) Jim playing hole 3. (RIGHT) Simon playing hole 3.

Jim nearly holes his birdie putt but walks off with a valuable par on a challenging hole.

What Went Wrong?

- Although both players were capable of hitting the required distance, Jim with a more consistent game, was much more likely to pull the shot off.
- Simon on the other hand should have played a five iron into the wide open area in front of the green, leaving himself a straightforward chip shot that doesn't require enormous skill. These two low-risk,

easy to execute shots would set up a one over par four or even a three if the chip was accurate.

Jim's preparation and execution were exemplary.

Hole 4.
Par 5. 525yd.

The longest hole on the course. The breeze is from the left and helping. Jim feels the breeze and thinks that if he can hit just a bit harder than normal he could get up in two. He decides to tee up on the left side of the tee

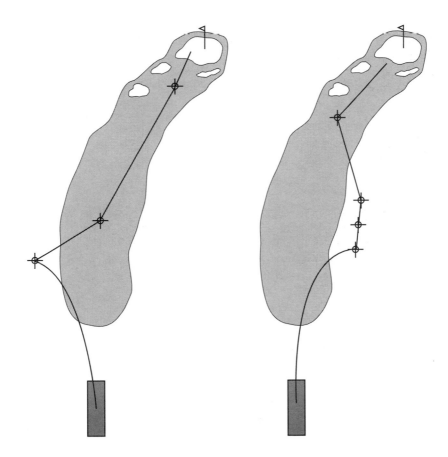

Fig 68 (LEFT) Jim playing hole 4. (RIGHT) Simon playing hole 4.

so that he can ride the wind for a few extra yards. Unfortunately, in his quest for power he tightens his grip on the club, closes the clubface on the backswing and hooks into the rough on the left hand side.

Simon again chooses his driver but doesn't allow for the wind and although well struck the ball curves into the right-hand rough. From this position and because it is a long hole, Simon selects his five wood and aims toward the flag in the distance. Unfortunately he tops the shot, it only travels 20yd and remains in the rough. He hurriedly advances to the ball and repeats, with uncanny precision, exactly the same shot. For his next shot he goes with his trusty seven iron and sensibly aims a few degrees to the left so that he can escape the rough. He hits a solid shot that travels a good distance along the fairway.

Over on the other side of the hole, Jim is cursing his bad luck. He has found a terrible lie in the rough. He is forced to hack the ball out onto the fairway leaving a shot of over 280yd remaining; now he can't reach the green in three. He hits a good five wood down the fairway.

Simon who is now playing his fifth shot has 150yd to the green. With the breeze helping, he takes a seven iron and despite an off-centre hit, gets the ball within a few feet of the green. From this position, although not on the putting surface, he uses his putter to good effect and gets down in two more shots for a seven.

Jim, feeling frustrated about the bad lie from two shots earlier, plays a sloppy wedge shot that only just catches the green. He proceeds to take three putts for a seven.

What Went Wrong?

- It was unrealistic for Jim to think that he could reach the green in two. This cocky strategy caused him to hook left – up until this point in the round he had hit each tee shot straight down the fairway. Also, he should have teed up on the right of the teeing ground so that he was angling slightly into the crosswind – this is an excellent safety measure. When he saw that his ball was lying poorly, he didn't accept that it was the punishment for a bad tee shot, instead he blamed bad luck. He then carried this frustration with him so that two shots later he hit his wedge so far from the hole that he three-putted.

- Simon played a driver from the tee when a three wood shot may have been safer, but his real mistake came on his second shot. He should have chosen a seven iron, his favourite club, and aimed out to the fairway, rather than hitting a wood from the rough and aiming at the green over 300yd away. He followed this course of action after he had hit two bad shots, when the damage was already done.

Summary

The examples given in these four holes are fairly typical of how golf is played. For Jim who swings well and hits mostly good shots, he scored four over par for the four holes played. If he is to reduce his handicap into single figures he will need to make better decisions and adopt a more consistent pre-shot routine. When he did this, on the par three hole for instance, he hit a superb shot. However, this is a common issue among many club players. If they want to play consistently, they need to think and prepare consistently. Jim also failed to stay in the present a couple of times contributing to poor shots.

Simon on the other hand doesn't hit the ball consistently so he needs to avoid taking on high-risk shots and instead select clubs that are easier to use. In short, he needs to play to his strengths.

Jack Nicklaus once said: 'If you are a thirty handicapper, then think like a thirty handicapper.' The message here is not to restrict your ambition, but rather to speed up your progress. Choose to take on shots that a thirty handicapper can play and leave the really tough shots to the low handicappers.

If Simon adopted this policy his scores would come tumbling down, and as he grows in confidence he would be able to gradually introduce more of the demanding shots.

ASSESSING YOUR OWN GAME

To be a good golfer it is essential that you know the strengths and weaknesses of your own game. This is especially valuable in terms of on-course shot selection where you need to know which parts of your game you can trust and therefore play them to your advantage. But also it is a requirement for improvement. If you cannot identify the areas that need to get better, then they are unlikely to get better on their own!

Strength and Weakness Analysis

Tournament professionals receive lots of statistics on their performance, these include:

- Stroke average
- Driving distance
- Driving accuracy
- Greens in regulation
- Putts per round
- Sand saves

This information helps them to accurately assess their game. For instance a player who is strong in driving distance and accuracy but weak in greens in regulation must be hitting too many poor iron shots, or playing too aggressively at the pin and not allowing enough margin for error. Either way, for this player to improve he would need to develop his iron play.

Complete the following exercise to **assess** your own game.

Listed are twenty-five different skills **and** characteristics involved in golf. Draw up **your** own chart like the one below, and place **the** following skills in the appropriate column; strength, weakness or in-between.

Driving Accuracy, Driving Distance
Fairway Woods, Long Irons
Mid Irons, Short Irons
Hitting a Draw, Hitting a Fade
High Shots, Low Shots
Club Selection
Pitching, Chipping
Greenside Bunker, Fairway Bunkers
Long Putts, Short Putts, Reading Greens
Escaping from Trouble
Course Management, Pre-shot Routine
Confidence, Visualization, Practice
Golf Specific Fitness

Weakness	In-between	Strength

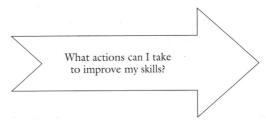

Fig 69 A simple way to analyze your game.

When you have completed your chart, consider what steps you could take over the next month to move one item, one column to the right. Here are some specific examples:

- Driving Distance – experiment with a different type of golf ball, or demo a new driver.
- Long Irons – visit the driving range on the next two Monday evenings and practise with the three, four and five iron. If you see no improvement then introduce more fairway wood shots to your game as these provide a similar distance and are generally easier to use.
- Short Putts – on the practice putting green, hole thirty consecutive putts from 3ft, if you miss on twenty-nine you have to start again. Stay until you have succeeded, even if you are late home for dinner.
- Escaping from Trouble – play nine holes and nominate it as a practice game. On each hole, hit a tee shot as normal but then pick up your ball and throw it into the rough or behind some trees. On a par three you may have hit the green so roll the ball off into a bunker. This form of practice will give you an excellent opportunity to improve your scrambling. Complete each hole in the lowest score you can. Repeat this nine-hole game as many times as you need, each time throwing the ball into the same place. In that way, you can measure your improvement as your scores get lower. (When using this form of on-course practice remember to follow golf etiquette.)
- Golf Specific Fitness – buy a book of stretching exercises for golf and spend fifteen minutes, three times a week working on them.

Other steps to take might include booking a golf lesson with your pro, watching a golf video or reading a book.

After the first month you will have seen an improvement, so then take another look at your strength and weakness chart and select another skill to develop in the second month, and so on.

Maintain the Strengths of Your Game

When targeting specific weaknesses, be sure not to neglect your strengths, these need to be maintained as they form the foundation of your game.

Know Your Distances

The majority of golfers now play by yardage. That is they use a course planner or distance markers along the hole for the exact yardage. This is a tremendous aid but to make good use of this information you do need to know how far you hit with each of your clubs. Finding out is a simple exercise.

Select ten balls of a similar type and quality to those that you regularly play. On a flat piece of ground hit all ten balls with one club, ignore the two shortest and two longest, and measure the distance to the centre of the other six balls. Repeat with an assortment of clubs: driver, five wood, four iron, six iron, eight iron and pitching wedge would give enough information to be able to fill in the remaining gaps. Record the figures and attach them to your bag for easy reference.

The considerations of wind direction, quality of the lie and elevation will all contribute to

An Easy Way to Remember Your Yardages

To help remember how far you hit with each club, write the figure on a narrow strip of paper and using clear tape attach it to the shaft of the club. Position it such that there is no distraction when you look down to hit a shot. This is perfectly acceptable within the Rules of Golf as long as you don't change the label during the course of play.

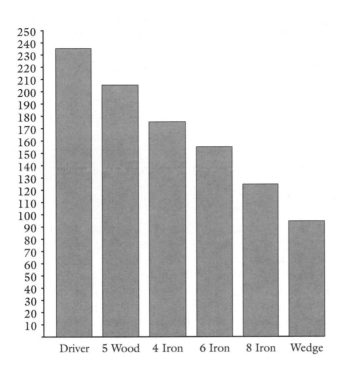

Fig 70
Typical
yardages for
a mid to
low-handicap
golfer.

your final club selection for any given shot, but the normal yardage is always the start point.

QUALITY PRACTICE

Standing on the practice range feels very different from standing on the golf course. Not only are the physical factors different – that is, the lie of the ball, but so too is the mental challenge. Hitting a bad shot on the range may just mean grabbing another ball and hitting it better; the golf course doesn't offer the same luxury. The majority of players hit the ball better in practice than on the course.

In practice, a typical golfer will adopt a very gung-ho attitude, swinging free and easy with no real care about the result. But when this same player arrives on the first tee he changes. As he tries to set everything in the perfect position, thinking through every moving part

of his swing, he can look like a statue over the ball. In part, practice is to condense what you know down to one or two simple thoughts that produce good consistent results.

If your practice is going to help your game it needs to prepare you for the feel of playing on the course. Making the decision to visit the driving range once a week and hit balls for an hour with no specific purpose would soon become boring and feel like a punishment.

To enjoy practice and for it to benefit your game consider the following points:

- Each session should have a specific purpose and give the player a sense of achievement.
- A practice schedule should cover a range of skills and shots that represent playing golf.
- It is essential to aim at a target. Shots need to be evaluated, without a target this is impossible.
- At least half of all practice shots should be

Fig 71 When possible, practise with a friend to add a competitive element to your practice.

played in a mode that simulates the feel of being on the course.

- Introduce a competitive element; practising with a partner is an excellent means of doing this. If you are practising alone then set personal goals and challenges.

When you visit the driving range are you practising to play better golf, or are you just hitting golf shots?

Sports psychologist, Dr Bob Rotella, encourages players to 'train and then trust' their game. Through good practice a player can repeat good habits such that they become grooved and can be relied upon to operate without conscious thought, thus becoming automatic. To arrive at this state requires that the player practise in a fashion that is similar

to the way they play, not completely different. In the short term, putting yourself under more pressure on the practice range may not produce better results, but it is giving you the skills to perform better where it counts most, on the course.

Practise with a Purpose

When you have assessed the strengths and weaknesses of your golf, you can practise with a purpose. Before you arrive at the range, decide how you are going to allocate your time. Here is an example of a useful session:

1. Warm up – simple stretching followed by ten gentle wedge shots (5 min).
2. Specific skill development – for example,

working on a grip change. A grip change is particularly challenging so the objective should be to adopt the correct grip on each shot rather than try to hit a good shot every time. A good shot is desirable and will become more frequent when the grip has improved (15 min).

3. Imagine you are playing golf – having practised your specific skill, now it is time to keep in touch with the rest of your game. Choose a target, select a club and using your normal on-course routine, execute the shot. Then for the next ball choose a different target and club. If you can visualize the holes of your own course, you can play an imaginary round of golf; hit a tee shot, estimate where it had finished and play the second shot from that position, include short approach shots and estimate how many putts. In this way you can compile a virtual score and this is practising to play golf! (15 min).

4. Finish feeling good – complete your session by hitting some of your favourite shots; this will ensure that you leave feeling good and therefore look forward to the next time you can practise (5 min).

Afterwards evaluate the session, enjoy a sense of achievement. If the session was poor, realize that tomorrow is a new day and it may be better. However, if several consecutive sessions are disappointing then seek help, make a lesson appointment or read a golf book, but do something about it.

A practice session of this type combines the training mode, when a new skill is being developed and the trusting mode when on-course play is rehearsed.

Practice is much more about quality than quantity, little and often suits most players. A very long practice session, if you are not used to it, can be harmful as tiredness and loss of interest create sloppy shots and despite huge

---

Playing an Imaginary Game of Golf

When practising an imaginary round of golf be disciplined with yourself. Golf is a one ball game. If you mishit a shot don't allow yourself to have another try, instead focus on the next shot and enjoy the challenge of playing a good recovery.

Practise like Tiger Woods

In his build-up to the US Open 2000 at Pebble Beach, Tiger Woods who knew the course well from many previous visits, practised at his home facility by visualizing every shot he was likely to play and executed each of those shots one hundred times. He went on to win by a record margin.

---

effort can soon turn into frustration. Many golfers have fallen victim to this unfortunate situation and as a result may have given up practice altogether. If you can relate to this, then consider a practice session similar to the one outlined above. Bring the enjoyment back and your game will benefit.

When practising chipping and pitching, only use a small number of balls. A great drill is to scatter ten balls around the practice green and treat each of them with the attention you would on the course and see how many shots it takes to hole out. Remember the number and next time try to beat it. Hitting a large bag of balls from one position encourages carelessness and feels nothing like the real thing.

When Your Practice Will Affect What You Practise

A practice session 30 min before you tee off in a competition needs to be in trusting not training mode. Venturing out onto the golf course with lots of swing thoughts in your mind is no way to play your best golf. Instead loosen up, rehearse your favourite shots and develop a positive feel. If you don't normally practise, it may be risky to do so before a big event. The temptation may be to start experimenting and unsettle your normal game. Most tournament players simply loosen up before play and then practise specific skills in training mode after they have completed their round.

If you are a keen competitor then winter practice may be the best time to make swing changes, during this period you would practise mainly in training mode. As the season draws closer then the balance would change to favour trusting mode.

Dividing up Practice Time

Finding a good balance to your practice is extremely worthwhile. Practising vigorously on shots that have little impact on your performance can create the impression that practice does not help.

Most golf experts if asked to nominate the three most valuable clubs in the bag would have the same answer: the driver, the wedge and the putter.

The Driver
Using your driving club well (driver or three wood) gives a golfer a great start point. A player feels confident when they have struck a good drive, while the player who is in trouble from the tee is always playing recovery golf and may feel like a second-class citizen.

The Wedge
Short iron shots from 50yd and less can set up realistic one-putt opportunities. A good wedge player will have less fear of missing the green on a long shot because they are confident of recovering.

The Putter
The most frequently used club in the set. All low scores will involve good putting.

On-Course Practice

An excellent way to practise is on course. Either playing on your own or with a partner, nominate a nine-hole game purely for practice. This creates an environment where it is possible to experiment in a fashion that might otherwise be impossible.

Decide on a specific objective, for example:

- Set the goal of positive thoughts only.
- Take special care to confirm how far you hit with particular clubs.
- If you play on a short course, tee off with a five iron to leave longer approach shots to the green.

This style of practice offers a stepping stone between the practice range and full-on competition.

(When using these forms of on course-practice remember to follow golf etiquette.)

Use the Monthly Practice Schedule (Fig 72) to divide up your practice time. If you practise for one hour each week or four hours each month that converts to sixteen practice sessions on the chart (each square represents a 15 min session). The shaded areas demonstrate a well-balanced schedule.

Limited Time to Practise
If other commitments limit the time that you spend on the practice range, don't despair. Practising at home or in the office can be very useful. Short putts can be grooved and using a mirror, set-up and swing positions can be checked. In addition, flicking through your 'Book of Good Shots', or visiting 'Your Personal Library', can raise your level of confidence and self-image as a golfer. Realize also, that many golfers who hit lots of practice balls may just be grooving their faults, unless they use the skills associated with quality practice.

Putting						
Chipping						
Pitching						
Bunkers						
Short Irons						
Mid Irons						
Long Irons						
Woods						

Fig 72 A Monthly Practice Schedule.

INTERESTING LIES AND SITUATIONS

The majority of golfers practise their shots on flat ground, either at their local club or nearby practice range where each ball has a perfect lie. One of the great features of playing on the golf course however, has to be the sheer variety of situations and lies that are encountered. While it would be nice to imagine your ball was only ever going to be hit from the tee, fairway or green, the reality is rather different.

Finding your ball in the rough is just one example of the variety of challenges you may encounter, and being able to *read* this situation to the extent that you can choose the correct club and possibly make suitable adjustments to your technique is a crucial skill.

Understanding the effect of a sloping lie is yet another example of a situation that requires a further adaptation of your skills and is of equal importance.

In addition, many golf courses have a wide variety of trees and bushes that aside from adding beauty and interest do, unfortunately, tend to get in the way! Learning to curve a shot around obstacles such as these is clearly a skill worth having and can be a lot of fun in the making.

Playing from the Rough

The difficulty when playing from the rough is that grass tends to get between club and ball at impact thus cushioning the blow. The key skill in this situation is to reduce the amount of grass causing the interference and to allow for the subsequent effect.

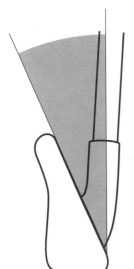
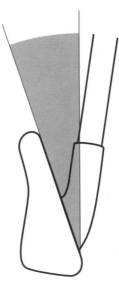

Fig 73 An iron will be de-lofted when the ball is positioned more towards the back foot.

A Long Shot from the Rough

The solution lies in creating a steeper angle of attack in order to contact the ball first. This can be achieved in the following way:

- Change your stance, move the ball back and the hands forward.
- Shift your weight more towards your left foot.
- On the backswing feel the arms swing up rather than the body turn around.

These adjustments have the effect of de-lofting the club with the result that the shot will tend to come out lower and roll further than normal.

A player with an in to out and shallow angle of attack will need to make a more exaggerated adjustment than the player with a naturally steep approach.

The Flyer.

This is a shot that flies further than expected because a small amount of grass gets trapped between club and ball; this fills the grooves on the face but does not cushion the power. Backspin on the shot is reduced and the ball flies off with little control.

Through trial and error learn to read a flying lie.

A further complication when using an iron to get out of the rough, is the fact that the longer grass tends to wrap itself around the clubface causing drag and distortion of the shot. An effective alternative to the iron, in these situations, is the use of the five or seven wood. The design of these clubs is such that aside from the more rounded nature of the head the sole is very often V-shaped thereby reducing the drag effect that is encountered with the elongated clubhead of an iron.

Be Realistic and Know Your Limitations

From the rough on a long hole it is very tempting to try and force a long shot. Learn to read the lie and know your limitations; it is often better to play a seven or eight iron down the fairway and leave a simple approach.

Rough around the Green

The same adjustments can be made although often the shot required needs to be high and soft rather than low and running. If this is the case, shots around the green can be played rather like a bunker shot, deliberately playing the grass and the ball together.

- Lay the clubface slightly open.
- Aim feet slightly left and position the ball towards the front foot.
- Use a longer swing allowing for the grass to cushion the shot and try to feel the back edge of the head bouncing rather than the front edge digging.

Use a Practice Swing to Help

When playing any shot from the rough, take several practice swings as part of your preparation. This will help you to feel the resistance of the grass and get a good feel for the adjustments you are making to stance and swing.

Please replace your divots afterwards.

Sloping Lies

There are four different types of sloping lie, uphill, downhill, ball above the feet and ball below the feet. Each one of these produces a predictable result and suitable adjustments can be made.

The general points to understand are:

1. The ball will tend to follow the slope – that is, from a downhill lie the ball will roll further so take a less powerful club, and from a lie with the ball above the feet, the ball will curve right to left so aim right to allow for it.
2. Gravity will be trying to push you down the slope so adopt a stance that facilitates good balance.

Uphill Lies

- Set the body perpendicular to the slope, body weight will be on the lower leg. This sets the body in a position where it can swing with the slope and not into it.
- Aim slightly to the right as the ball tends to hook.
- The slope will add height but lose distance so select a more powerful club.

Downhill Lies

- Set the body perpendicular to the slope, body weight will be on the lower leg. This sets the body in a position where it can swing with the slope and not into it.
- Position the ball a little further back in the stance.
- During the downswing make a special effort to stay with the shot, try to feel the club follow the contour of the slope especially just after impact.
- A well-struck shot will travel lower and further so use a weaker club.

Club Selection from a Downhill Lie

Long irons are extremely difficult to use from a downhill lie because the club loft is reduced. However, a middle iron will travel much further than normal, so there is no need to be greedy.

Fig 74 Aim to the right when the ball is above your feet.

Ball above Feet

- Adopt a spine angle that maintains the same relationship to the slope, as a normal stance would have to level ground. This means your posture will be more vertical.
- Grip down the club and stand further away.
- Aim to the right, as the ball will hook.

Ball below Feet

- Adopt a spine angle that maintains the same relationship to the slope, as a normal stance would have to level ground. This means your posture will be more bent forward.
- Grip at the very top of the handle and stand closer.
- Aim left, as the ball will slice.

From any sloping lie, balance will be the greatest challenge. When you play the shot, swing easy.

MAKING THE BALL CURVE (DELIBERATELY)

Occasionally an obstacle may block the route to the hole. Dependent on the player's standard he may decide to play safe or deliberately curve the ball using a controlled hook or slice. This creativity comes from the basic principles of ball flight as covered in Chapter 3.

The good news is that the shot can be predetermined by the start position. The simple requirement is to aim the clubface where the ball needs to finish and aim the body where the ball needs to start.

A Controlled Hook
The clubface has to be closed in relation to the swing path so imparting a right to left spin.

- Aim the face at the target
- Aim your feet, hips and shoulders to the right and then take your grip. The grip will feel rotated to the right of the centre line of the club.
- Swing as normal and the ball will hook.

A hook hits the ball with a lower and longer trajectory; a seven iron may travel as far as a normal five iron.

A Controlled Slice
The clubface has to be open in relation to the swing path so imparting a left to right spin.

- Aim the face at the target.
- Aim your feet, hips and shoulders to the left and then take your grip. The grip will feel rotated to the left of the centre line of the club.
- Swing as normal and the ball will slice.

Fig 75 Aim the clubface where the ball needs to finish and align the body where the ball needs to start.

A slice shot will fly higher and shorter so use a stronger club.

A word of warning: When playing a slice shot, remember the ball will climb very quickly, so if you are playing around trees take care not to hit any overhanging branches.

High and Low Shots

The High Shot
This shot requires that the clubface arrive at impact in a more lofted position and as with the controlled hook and slice, this can be pre-set in the start position.

- Position the ball 2in more forward than normal.
- Sit your body weight over the back foot.
- Make a normal backswing but finish with a high followthrough.

The high shot is more difficult to execute than the low one. Due to the adjustments, there is a very real danger of hitting the ground before the ball and losing distance. Try this shot in practice and only use it on course when you feel you have mastered it.

The Low Shot
This may be the shot of choice when faced with hitting under an obstacle or playing into a stiff breeze. A low shot needs the clubface to be de-lofted at impact.

- Position the ball 2in further back than normal.
- Allow body weight to favour the left foot.
- Use a three-quarter length backswing with a short followthrough.

To keep the ball low, avoid hitting too hard, especially into the wind. Hitting hard increases the amount of backspin on the ball, which makes it climb. Therefore club selection is crucial; pick two clubs extra and play it easy, this imparts much less backspin so the ball will stay low.

High and Low Shots with a Wood
The high and low shots described above relate to iron shots; changing the trajectory on a wood is extremely difficult. Try the following;

Find the Correct Trajectory

If you are unsure about the trajectory of a certain club try this method. Lay the club on the ground with the grip end pointing towards your target. Now stand on the clubface so that the shaft rises off the ground. This angle is a good guide to the amount of loft on the club and the trajectory that you can expect from it. Use this technique when you need to go under or over an obstruction.

---

1. Into wind the temptation is to hit harder; this tends to put more backspin on the ball and send it high, so try to hit easier than normal.
2. On a downwind shot use a more lofted club, that is, a three wood instead of a driver, this will give the ball more airtime and more distance.

DEALING WITH THE WEATHER

Part of the challenge of golf is the weather, especially in the British Isles. The oldest courses in the land, those situated by the sea, rely on the wind as their main form of defence. As such the elements are a hazard and should be viewed in the same light as bunkers and ponds.

Tom Watson, winner of five British Opens, once said: 'I love rotten weather. The founders of the game accepted nature for what it gave, or what it took away. Wind and rain are great challenges. They separate real golfers.'

Equipment

As any good boy scout would tell you 'Be prepared'. To play the best you can in cold and or wet conditions you need to be warm and dry.

Here is a list of useful items:

- Golf shoes – waterproof and breathable with interchangeable spikes, metal spikes for winter, soft rubber for summer.
- Waterproof suit – waterproof and breathable, and don't just save it for a rainy day. A good suit will keep you warm and won't restrict your swing.
- All-weather glove – maintains grip even when clubs are wet. Have a couple of spare gloves in your bag so you can change to a

dry one every few holes (keep these in a plastic bag so they don't get wet).

- An umbrella.
- A towel – to clean and dry your clubs. When it is raining keep the towel dry, either hook it under your umbrella or tuck it in a pocket of your bag.
- A hood for your bag – most bags come complete with a rainhood, if not they can be purchased separately.
- Headwear – visor, cap and bobble hat.
- Hands – mittens and/or pocket warmer.
- Lightweight golf bag – in the winter when the use of trolleys is frequently prohibited, so have a light carry bag available, preferably one that incorporates a simple stand.
- Fairway woods – when the ground is soft, a fairway wood is easier to use than a long iron that has less bounce and may dig in.
- Tacky grips – worn grips will slip especially in wet weather. New grips are very inexpensive and make your clubs feel like new.

Playing in the Wind

Many players underestimate the effect of the wind. For every 5–10mph adjust your club selection by one and remember the old adage 'when it's breezy, swing easy'.

Downwind
Playing downwind is generally easier. The ball goes further from the tee shot and the approach will require a shorter club. Also any curve will be straightened out, so if you usually aim left to allow for a slice, with the wind behind aim a little straighter than normal. Shots to the green will tend to run on so allow for this in your club selection.

Against the Wind
Making too many adjustments when playing into the wind can produce mishits, so accept

that the hole will play longer. Last week you may have reached with a drive and a seven iron, but that was 10mph downwind, now it is 20mph against. Be realistic!

Any curve in flight will be exaggerated, so if you aim left with a slice allow a little extra and remember to aim the clubface left and not just your feet. Select a longer club that you think will go past the flag as most shots come up short.

Crosswind
The simplest way of dealing with a crosswind is to play with it. That is, to realize the ball will be affected and allow for it in your aim. The alternative is to change from your normal shot and fight the wind but this is more likely to produce an error.

If you play with a left to right shot and the wind is from the right your flight will be neutralized and may curve very little, so there is no need to aim as far left as normal. If however the wind is from the left then you will have to aim well left, as the curve will be greater.

Slicing in the Wind

A wind that is blowing from the left and against will produce the most curve on a slice shot, while a wind from the right and behind will do its best to straighten any slice.

When playing a tree-lined course there will be many places where you are sheltered and cannot feel the wind. Using the map on the scorecard, draw a large arrow indicating wind direction – on an inland course this will rarely change during a game and you can refer to it when you are in a sheltered area.

Playing in the Rain

To perform well in the rain is all about two words, perseverance and attitude. The whole

The Best Advice for Playing in the Wind

My best advice when playing into the wind is simply to do your best to hit a good solid shot and my best advice when playing downwind is simply to do your best to hit a good solid shot!

process may feel uncomfortable, you may just want to get it over with as fast as possible, but if you are competing then you want to do the best you can. Many of your fellow competitors will let their heads drop and throw in the towel, so in bad conditions the number of real opponents that you need to beat is far less than on a beautiful sunny day. Keep yourself positive by realizing that a good score in tough conditions is different from a good score in easy conditions, so be realistic, and raise your level of acceptance. Be prepared to hit fewer sweet shots than normal, just try to advance it along and get the job done.

Do:

- Keep your grips dry and wear an all weather glove.

- Put on waterproof clothing and use an umbrella.
- Base your club selection on trying to reach the back edge of the green, because a ball with less than perfect contact may still finish on the putting surface.
- Choose fairway woods rather than long irons.
- Enjoy the challenge of building a score in adverse conditions.
- Value your short game skills.

Don't:

- Let other players' club selection influence you.
- Choose to play high-risk shots.
- Expect perfection.

To Keep You Going in the Rain

When playing in the rain remind yourself of Tom Watson's statement (cited in this chapter) and allow the elements to identify you as a real golfer.

CHAPTER 6

Fitness for Golf

Traditionally golf has not been seen as an activity that requires an outstanding level of fitness. However, at the highest levels of competitive play it is increasingly the case that players are working on their fitness and reaping the benefit. Mobile fitness centres allowing players access to specialist equipment now support the major tours. The benefit of a good fitness programme for a top player is not just about improving physical fitness, but reducing the chance of injury and enabling the player to extend his career over a longer period.

The three key elements are: endurance, strength and flexibility.

Endurance

Both cardiovascular and muscular endurance are important to the accomplished golfer who is practising and playing on a regular basis. An average golfer playing one round per week may not need to concern himself with improving endurance to any great extent, although it would obviously be of benefit to his golf and his personal esteem. Improved endurance increases a golfer's capacity for work without feeling the effects of tiredness. The improved efficiency of the heart and lungs in supplying blood will cause less exertion to the player.

Two of the best exercises for endurance are walking briskly or riding a bike.

Strength

Muscles provide the power in the golf swing and so it is important to have sufficient muscular strength to generate the required clubhead speed at impact. This strength also provides a golfer with much of the control required in swinging the clubhead.

To increase strength, training programmes will involve muscles being loaded with high-repetition, low-resistance exercises. An increase of strength in the relevant muscle groups provides the source of more power. In general the areas to develop are the hands, forearms, trunk rotators, back, abdomen and legs.

Flexibility

Having strength without flexibility is of no value. A heavily muscled body-builder may be very strong, but his short muscles would make it difficult for him to generate a powerful golf swing. Instead, specific stretching and mobility exercises will improve the capacity to create a powerful rotation of the body whilst maintaining control and balance.

Flexibility is important to golfers of all ages and ability. Often players are trying to achieve swing positions that are simply impossible without developing a wider range of movement. Stretching exercises should be performed with smooth movements and held for around ten seconds. Avoid bouncing in and out of a position as this may cause injury.

Warming Up

Whether a player is involved in a specialist exercise programme or not, warming up before practice or play is highly recommended. This reduces the chance of injury and prepares your body for action. Many average players get to the first tee with no preparation, take hold of their driver, have a couple of violent practice swings and then hit. On a cold day this can be especially dangerous.

The four exercises below offer a simple warm-up routine. Hold each position for a few seconds and repeat twice. Don't tense the muscles and tendons until they hurt, instead stay relaxed and keep breathing.

Shoulder Stretch
Take hold of a club with one hand at each end. Raise the club above your head and gently stretch your arms backwards. Hold for ten seconds and repeat.

Fig 76a Shoulder stretch.

Quad Stretch

Standing on one leg, pull the other foot up towards your backside. Hold for ten seconds, repeat and then change legs. Use a club for balance.

Thigh Stretch

Hold a club across your shoulders and assume good golf posture. From this position, lower yourself by bending your knees. Hold for five seconds and repeat.

Hamstring Stretch

Cross legs and bend forward. Stretch as low as you can and hold for ten seconds. Repeat and then change legs.

Fig 76b Quad stretch.

Fig 76c Thigh stretch.

Fig 76d Hamstring stretch.

CHAPTER 7

Summary

This book has attempted to present the skills of golf in a fashion that is straightforward to follow and enjoyable to read. The main message is that to develop their standard of play, a golfer will benefit from stepping back and taking an overview of their individual approach to the game. In particular, to see the game in the light of the 'Triangle of Success':

1. Long Game Skills
2. Short Game Skills
3. On-Course Skills

Fig 77 The Triangle of Success.

Regardless of your current level of experience or standard of play, improvement will be more forthcoming if you spend time on each of these crucial departments. However, the balance of time spent on each element will vary from player to player.

The beginner is well advised to concentrate on long game skills with a steady increase in short game development. Once able to hit around 50 per cent of practice shots with a reasonable result they should then begin to consider on-course skills in more detail.

The experienced golfer who plays regularly and hits the ball with a good level of consistency, will probably benefit by spending the majority of their practice time focused on the short game and on-course skills. For players in this category, a change of technique or any extra practice in these two areas is likely to lower their scores more quickly than any long game change. Remember that just visiting the golf range and hitting fifty consecutive shots with a driver in a totally gung-ho fashion, does little to recreate the on-course conditions of playing golf. Consider any practice session as a dress rehearsal and appreciate that the better you practice, the better you will play.

Further help

To help develop your game further, book a lesson with a PGA Professional. It is important to find someone with whom you can connect and whose style of teaching matches your style of learning. For instance, do you learn best from detailed explanation or do you prefer simple descriptions with lots of demonstration. Do you respond most effectively to what you hear, what you see or what you feel? As an individual, each golfer will have their own preference and most experienced instructors will be able to get the message across using a number of different styles.

When you have found a 'Pro' that you feel comfortable with, then make a commitment to a series of lessons, including a session to the course. This will allow him to get a good understanding for the three elements of your 'Golf Triangle' and give you great advice and support to improve them.

What Does Golf Have to Offer?

Any personal review should include taking a look at the wide array of pleasures that golf has to offer and deciding whether you could gain even more enjoyment. To help here are a few features that golfers can enjoy when playing this great game:

- The comradeship shared with playing partners and opponents alike. The sportsmanship and standard of behaviour passed down through previous generations is *the responsibility of all golfers* to maintain and feel proud about.
- The sense of personal achievement when posting a good score.
- The scenic beauty and natural wildlife that are an integral part of any course.
- The opportunity to escape from the pressures of everyday life.
- Golf is a game for a lifetime and it can be enjoyed by all generations.
- It is a family game that can accommodate the needs of children, parents and grandparents on the same stage.
- Fresh air and a brisk walk provide very good exercise.

- The handicap system that allows all players to compete on level terms.
- The simple joy of striking a sweet shot.

Learn to Play with a Good Attitude

The only person who stands between you and full enjoyment from golf, is you. Be realistic with your expectations and accept that playing a round of golf will involve hitting bad shots, that's why you have a handicap. Even if you play off scratch or better, having a realistic level of acceptance is crucial because it allows you to see things in a balanced way and move on. For example, statistics from professional golf tournaments show that from a distance of 6ft, 50 per cent of putts miss. These putts are being hit on perfect greens with the best equipment, preparation and advice available. It would therefore be unrealistic to expect to hole every 6ft putt in the November Monthly Medal at your home club. In this example, the player who gets mad after missing twice would be in danger of allowing his emotions to spill over into the 'I'll never hole a putt' attitude, and once he begins to think that, he will be right. The player who can stay patient and maintain control of his emotions is far more likely to hole the six footers that present themselves later in the round.

This attitude does not mean that bad shots should be tolerated, but instead, they should be dealt with at a different time. A time that is not going to hurt your current game. This time should be in practice, not in live competition.

To share in the pleasures that golf has to offer always try to enjoy the good shots and don't dwell on the bad ones. Play to your strengths and act in a manner that upholds the very best traditions of the game.

Good luck and best wishes.

Fig 78 The author working with England Boys player Chris Mayson.

Glossary of Golfing Terms

Ace. A hole in one.

Address. The position of the club and the player in relation to the ball when preparing to play a shot.

Air shot. A stroke that fails to make contact with the ball.

Albatross. A score on one hole of three under par – i.e. a two on a par five.

Alignment. The aim of a player's body and club in relation to the target.

Amateur. A golfer who plays the game with no income benefit.

Approach. A shot played towards the green.

Apron. The grass area around the green that is cut shorter than the fairway, but not as short as the green itself.

Arc. The path of the clubhead during the golf swing.

Back 9. The holes numbered 10 to 18 on an 18-hole golf course.

Backspin. The backward rotation of a golf ball that causes it to fly high and grip when landing on the ground.

Ball mark. The indentation that a ball makes when landing on the soft surface of the green.

Ball to target line. An imaginary straight line running from the ball to the target and from the ball away from the target.

Birdie. A score of one under par for the hole.

Bogey. A score of one over par for the hole.

Borrow. In putting the amount of compensation made by a player to allow for any side slopes, gravity or grain on the surface of the green.

Boundary. The perimeter of a golf course. Outside this perimeter is called 'Out of Bounds'.

Break. The amount of curvature a ball takes when struck towards the hole on the green.

Bunker. A hollow or depression in the ground generally filled with sand.

Caddy. A person who carries a golfer's clubs.

Carry. The distance the ball travels through the air from where it is played originally to where it lands.

Casual water. Temporary accumulation of water that is not part of the normal hazards of the golf course.

Chip. A low flighted mainly running shot around the green.

Choke down. To grip lower down the handle for greater control.

Closed clubface. The toe of the club is turned inward making the clubface aim left of the target.

Closed address. When a player's body and feet aim to the right of the target.

Dimples. The indentations on a ball that help create its flight.

Divot. A small piece of turf removed when playing a shot.

Dogleg. A hole which bends either to the right or left.

Downswing. The part of the swing where the club is moving toward the ball.

Draw. A ball that curves slightly right to left in flight.

Drop. The action a player takes in returning a ball into play having taken relief or a penalty.

Duff. A term used for a very badly struck shot.

Eagle. A score on one hole of two under par – i.e. a three on a par five.

Etiquette. The good behaviour and conduct expected of all golfers.

Explosion shot. The shot made from a buried lie in a bunker in which the club digs down and displaces a considerable amount of sand.

Fade. A ball that curves slightly left to right in flight.

Fairway. A closely mowed part of a hole between the tee and the green.

Fat. A term used to describe a shot where the club makes contact with the ground before the ball.

Flagstick. The stick, usually with a flag attached to it, placed in the hole to make its location visible from a distance. Also called the 'pin'.

Flex. The bend of the golf shaft during the swing.

Flier. When a ball flies quicker than expected and with less control, usually from a semi-rough or a grassy lie.

Flight. The path or trajectory of the golf ball through the air.

Fore. The traditional shout to warn golfers that the ball is travelling in their direction.

Grain. The direction in which grass grows or lies on the putting green.

Green Fee. The fee charged by a golf club to a visiting golfer.

Grip. Either the handle of the golf club or the way the hands are positioned onto that handle.

GUR. Ground Under Repair. Any part of a golf course stipulated as unfit for play, from which a free drop is permitted.

Half. A drawn hole or match.

Handicap. A scoring adjustment based on ability.

Hazard. Any bunker, ditch, pond, stream or lake as defined by a golf club.

Heel. The portion of the clubface that is located towards the hosel.

Hole in one. When a tee shot goes directly into the hole.

Honour. The privilege of playing first from the tee.

Hook. A ball that curves severely from right to left.

Hosel. The part of the clubhead to which the shaft is fitted. Sometimes referred to as the neck.

Impact. The moment in time that the clubface contacts the ball.

Lag. A putt – usually of significant length – that stops close enough to the hole to allow a tap in.

Lateral water hazard. When water lies parallel to the line of play rather than across it. Marked with red stakes.

Lie. Position of the ball in relation to the ground.

Line. The direction in which a shot or putt should be taken in relation to the hole.

Lip. The edge of the hole.

Lob. A high soft-flighted shot similar to a pitch.

Lob wedge. A club that is more lofted than a sand wedge.

Local knowledge. A benefit gained by a player when playing his own course.

Local rules. Those rules that appertain to the individual club itself.

Loft. The amount of angle built into the clubface to help elevate the ball.

Lost ball. When a ball cannot be found within five minutes of searching for it, it is deemed lost.

Marker. A coin or disc used to mark the position of the ball on the green. Also a fellow competitor or scorer who records the players' scores. Also objects on the teeing ground defining the area from which to play.

Open. With regard to the clubface, open means the face aims to the right of target.

Out of bounds. When a ball goes beyond the boundaries of the golf course.

Par. The assessed standard score for a hole based on length and difficulty.

Penalty stroke. A stroke or strokes added to a score because of the breach of the rules of golf.

Pitch. A relatively high shot played when approaching the green.

Pitch and run. Similar to pitch but with a lower trajectory.

Pitch mark. The indentation that a ball makes when landing on the soft surface of the green.

Pivot. The turning action of the body around a fixed axis during the backswing.

Plane. Swing plane. The angle of the swing based on the player's height, posture and the club in use.

Plugged ball. A ball that remains in its own depression on landing.

Provisional ball. A second ball played from the same spot as the original when the original ball may be lost or out of bounds.

Pull. A shot that travels in a straight line, but to the left of target.

Push. A shot that travels in a straight line, but to the right of target.

Rough. The longer grass area bordering the fairways.

R & A. The Royal and Ancient Golf Club of St Andrews.

Semi-Rough. A strip of grass that lies between the fairway and longer rough.

Shank. A ball that is struck from the hosel of an iron club and travels to the right.

Slice. A ball that curves severely from left to right.

Sole. The bottom of the clubhead.

Splash. The usual term for playing a normal bunker shot.

Square. When the clubface is at right angles to the target line.

Stance. The position of the feet when the player addresses the ball.

Stroke. Any forward movement of the club made with the intention of hitting the ball.

Takeaway. The first few inches of the back-swing movement.

Teeing ground. An area of two club lengths in depth, the front and sides of which are defined by tee-markers.

Tee peg. The small implement on which to place the ball when commencing a hole.

Thin. A shot that is struck from the bottom edge of the golf club.

Through the Green. All parts of a hole except the hazards, teeing ground or the green.

Toe. The end of the clubface that is opposite to the heel.

Trajectory. The flight and path of the golf ball through the air.

Unplayable lie. Any place on the course, except in a hazard, that the player chooses not to play his ball from. The decision results in a one-stroke penalty.

USGA. The United States Golf Association.

Winter rules. Preferred lies. Played through-out the winter to allow players to clean and place their ball due to adverse ground conditions.

Yardage charts. Course planners. The lay-out and design of golf holes with lengths measured from important features on each hole to help the players judge which club they need to play.

Bibliography

Williams, K., The Golf Workshop (Crowood Press, 1998)

Jacobs, J., *The Golf Swing Simplified* (Stanley Paul & Co, 1993)

Pelz, D., *Dave Pelz's Short Game Bible* (Broadway Books, 1999)

Rotella, R., *Golf is Not a Game of Perfect* (Simon & Schuster, 1995)

Cochran, A. and J. Stobbs, *Search for the Perfect Swing* (The Golf Society of Great Britain, 1968)

Index

INDEX